Kant's Critical Philosophy

The Doctrine of the Faculties

Kant's Critical Philosophy

The Doctrine of the Faculties

Gilles Deleuze

Translated by
Hugh Tomlinson and Barbara Habberjam

UNIVERSITY OF MINNESOTA PRESS
Minneapolis

Orginally published in France in 1963 as
La Philosophie Critique de Kant by Presses Universitaires de France.

The Publishers acknowledge the financial assistance of the French Ministry of Culture and Communication in the translation of this work.

Published by the University of Minnesota Press,
2037 University Avenue Southeast, Minneapolis MN 55414

Printed in the United States

Library of Congress Cataloging in Publication Data

Deleuze, Gilles.
Kant's critical philosophy.

Translation of: La philosophie critique de Kant.
Includes index.
1. Kant, Immanuel, 1724–1804—Knowledge, Theory of.
2. Knowledge, Theory of—History—18th century. I. Title.
B2799.K7D4313 1984 121 84-7548
ISBN 0-8166-1341-9
ISBN 0-8166-1436-9 (pbk.)

Contents

Preface

Gilles Deleuze

On four poetic formulas which might summarize the Kantian philosophy

I

The first is Hamlet's great formula, 'The time is out of joint'. Time is out of joint, time is unhinged. The hinges are the axis around which the door turns. *Cardo*, in Latin, designates the subordination of time to the cardinal points through which the periodical movements that it measures pass. As long as time remains on its hinges, it is subordinate to movement: it is the measure of movement, interval or number. This was the view of ancient philosophy. But time out of joint signifies the reversal of the movement–time relationship. It is now movement which is subordinate to time. Everything changes, including movement. We move from one labyrinth to another. The labyrinth is no longer a circle, or a spiral which would translate its complications, but a thread, a straight line, all the more mysterious for being simple, inexorable as Borges says, 'the labyrinth which is composed of a single straight line, and which is indivisible, incessant'. Time is no longer related to the movement which it measures, but movement is related to the time which conditions it: this is the first great Kantian reversal in the *Critique of Pure Reason.*

Time is no longer defined by succession because succession concerns only things and movements which are in time. If time itself were succession, it would need to succeed in another time, and on to infinity. Things succeed each other in various times, but they are also simultaneous in the same time, and they remain in an indefinite time. It is no longer a question of defining time by succession, nor space by simultaneity, nor permanence by eternity. Permanence, succession and simultaneity are modes and relationships of time. Thus, just as time can no longer be defined by succession, space cannot be defined by coexistence. Both space and time have to find completely new determinations. Everything which moves and changes is in time, but time itself does not change, does not move, any more than it is eternal. It is the form of everything that changes and moves, but it is an immutable Form which does not change. It is not an eternal form, but in fact the form of that which is *not* eternal, the immutable form of change and movement. Such an autonomous form seems to indicate a profound mystery: it demands a new definition of time which Kant must discover or create.

II

'I is another': this formula from Rimbaud can be seen as the expression of another aspect of the Kantian revolution, again in the *Critique of Pure Reason*. It is the most difficult aspect. Indeed, Kant explains that the Ego[1] itself is in time, and thus constantly changing: it is a passive, or rather receptive, Ego, which experiences changes in time. But, on the other hand, the I[1] is an act which constantly carries out a synthesis of time, and of that which happens in time, by dividing up the present, the past and the future at every instant. The I and the Ego are thus separated by the line of time which relates them to each other, but under the condition of a fundamental difference. So that my existence can never be determined as that of an active and spontaneous being. We cannot say with Descartes, 'I think, therefore I am. I am a thing that thinks.' If it is true that the *I think* is a determination, it implies in this respect an indeterminate existence (*I am*). But nothing so far tells us under what form this existence is determined by the *I think*: it is determinable only in time, under the form of time, thus as the existence of a phenomenal, receptive and changing ego. I cannot therefore constitute myself as a unique and active subject, but as a passive ego which represents to itself only the activity of its own thought; that is to say, the *I*, as an Other which affects it. I am separated from myself by the form of time, and nevertheless I am one, because the *I* necessarily affects this form by carrying out its synthesis and because the Ego is necessarily affected as content in this form. The form of the determinable means that the determined ego represents determination as an Other. It is like a double diversion of the I and the Ego in the time which relates them to each other, stitches them together. It is the thread of time.

In one sense, Kant goes further than Rimbaud. For Rimbaud's famous formula 'I is another' relates back strangely to an Aristotelian way of thinking: 'Too bad for the wood which finds itself a violin! if the copper wakes up a bugle, that is not its fault' . . . For Rimbaud, it is thus a question of the determining form of a thing in so far as it is distinguished from the matter in which it is embodied: a mould as in Aristotle. For Kant, it is a question of the form of time in general, which distinguishes between the act of the I, and the ego to which this act is attributed: an infinite modulation, no longer a mould. Thus time moves into the subject, in order to distinguish the Ego from the I in it. It is the form under which the I affects the ego, that is, the way in which the mind affects itself. It is in this sense that time as immutable form, which could no longer be defined by simple succession, appeared as the form of interiority (inner sense), whilst space, which could no longer be defined by coexistence, appeared for its part as the form of exteriority. 'Form of interiority' means not only that time is internal to us, but that our interiority constantly divides us from ourselves, splits us in two: a splitting in two which never runs its course, since time has no end. A giddiness, an oscillation which constitutes time.

III

The third aspect of the Kantian revolution concerns the *Critique of Practical Reason*, and might appear in formulas akin to those of Kafka. 'The Good is what the Law says' . . . '*The* law' is already a strange expression, from the point of view of philosophy which only scarcely knew *laws*. This is clear in antiquity, notably in Plato's *Politics*. If men knew what Good was, and knew how to conform to it, they would not need laws. Laws, or the law, are only a 'second resort', a representative of the Good in a world deserted by the gods. When the true politics is absent, it leaves general directives according to which men must conduct themselves. Laws are therefore, as it were, the imitation of the Good which serves as their highest principle. They derive from the Good under certain conditions.

When Kant talks about the law, it is, on the contrary, as the highest instance. Kant reverses the relationship of the law and the Good, which is as important as the reversal of the movement–time relationship. It is the Good which depends on the law, and not vice versa. In the same way as the objects of knowledge revolve around the subject (*I*), the Good revolves around the subjective law. But what do we mean by 'subjective' here? The law can have no content other than itself, since all content of the law would lead it back to a Good whose imitation it would be. In other words, the law is pure form and has no object: neither sensible nor intelligible. It does not tell us *what* we must do, but to what (subjective) rule we must conform, whatever our action. Any action is moral if its maxim can be thought without contradiction as universal, and if its motive has no other object than this maxim. For example, the lie cannot be thought as formally universal without contradiction, since it at least implies people who believe in it, and who, in believing in it, are not lying. The moral law is thus defined as the pure form of universality. The law does not tell us which object the will must pursue to be good, but the form which it must take in order to be moral. The law as empty form in the *Critique of Practical Reason* corresponds to time as pure form in the *Critique of Pure Reason*. The law does not tell us *what* we must do, it merely tells us 'you must!', leaving us to deduce from it the Good, that is, the object of this pure imperative. But it is the Good which derives from the law, and not vice versa. As in

Kafka's *The Penal Colony*, it is a determination which is purely practical and not theoretical. The law is not known, since there is nothing in it to 'know'. We come across it only through its action, and it acts only through its sentence and its execution. It is not distinguishable from the sentence, and the sentence is not distinguishable from the application. We know it only through its imprint on our heart and our flesh: we are guilty, necessarily guilty. Guilt is like the moral thread which duplicates the thread of time.

IV

'A disorder of all the senses', as Rimbaud said, or rather an unregulated exercise of all the faculties. This might be the fourth formula of a deeply romantic Kant in the *Critique of Judgement*. In the two other Critiques, the various subjective faculties had entered into relationships with each other, but these relationships were rigorously regulated in so far as there was always a dominant or determining faculty which imposed its rule on the others. There were several of these faculties: external sense, inner sense, imagination, understanding, reason, each well-defined. But in the *Critique of Pure Reason* the understanding was dominant because it determined inner sense through the intermediary of a synthesis of the imagination, and even reason submitted to the role which was assigned to it by the understanding. In the *Critique of Practical Reason*, reason was dominant because it constituted the pure form of universality of the law, the other faculties following as they might (the understanding applied the law, the imagination received the sentence, the inner sense felt the consequences or the sanction). But we see Kant, at an age when great writers rarely have anything new to say, confronting a problem which is to lead him into an extraordinary undertaking: if the faculties can, in this way, enter into relationships which are variable, but regulated by one or other of them, it must follow that all together they are capable of relationships which are free and *unregulated*, where each goes to its own limit and nevertheless shows the possibility of some sort of harmony with the others . . . Thus we have the *Critique of Judgement* as foundation of Romanticism.

It is no longer the aesthetic of the *Critique of Pure Reason*, which considered the sensible as a quality which could be related to an object in space and in time; it is not a logic of the sensible, nor even a new *logos* which would be time. It is an aesthetic of the Beautiful and of the Sublime, in which the sensible is valid in itself and unfolds in a *pathos* beyond all logic, which will grasp time in its surging forth, in the very origin of its thread and its giddiness. It is no longer the Affect of the *Critique of Pure Reason*, which related the Ego to the *I* in a relationship which was still regulated by the order of time: it is a Pathos which leaves them to evolve freely in order to form strange combinations as sources of time; 'arbitrary forms of possible intuitions'.

What is in question in the *Critique of Judgement* is how certain phenomena which come to define the Beautiful give an autonomous supplementary dimension to the inner sense of time, a power of free reflection to the imagination, an infinite conceptual power to the understanding. The various faculties enter into an accord which is no longer determined by any one of them, and which is all the deeper because it no longer has any rule, and because it demonstrates a spontaneous accord of the Ego and the *I* under the conditions of a beautiful Nature. The Sublime goes even further in this direction: it brings the various faculties into play in such a way that they struggle against one another, the one pushing the other towards its maximum or limit, the other reacting by pushing the first towards an inspiration which it would not have had alone. Each pushes the other to the limit, but each makes the one go beyond the limit of the other. It is a terrible struggle between imagination and reason, and also between understanding and the inner sense, a struggle whose episodes are the two forms of the Sublime, and then Genius. It is a tempest in the depths of a chasm opened up in the subject. The faculties confront one another, each stretched to its own limit, and find their accord in a fundamental discord: a discordant accord is the great discovery of the *Critique of*

Judgement, the final Kantian reversal. Separation which reunites was Kant's first theme, in the *Critique of Pure Reason*. But at the end he discovers discord which produces accord. An unregulated exercise of all the faculties, which was to define future philosophy, just as for Rimbaud the disorder of all the senses was to define the poetry of the future. A new music as discord, and as a discordant accord, the source of time.

That is why I have suggested four formulas which are clearly arbitrary in relation to Kant, but not at all arbitrary in relation to what Kant has left us for the present and the future. De Quincey's admirable essay *The Last days of Emmanuel Kant* summed it all up, but only the reverse side of things which find their development in the four poetic formulas of Kantianism. Could this be a Shakespearian side of Kant, a kind of *King Lear*?

1 Translators' Note: The French terms 'je' and 'moi', although literally meaning 'I' and 'me', have been rendered as 'I' and 'the ego' throughout as conveying more effectively the distinction which Deleuze wishes to draw.

Translators' Introduction

The present work was Gilles Deleuze's third book, first published in 1963 as part of the Presses Universitaires de France 'Le Philosophe' series of introductions to individual philosophers. As an essay on Kant it is remarkable. While the standard English introductions (and commentaries) concentrate almost exculsively on the *Critique of Pure Reason*, Deleuze surveys the entire critical philosophy in just over a hundred pages of original French text. Not only does he summarize the essential theme of each of the three Critiques, he also gives a clear and original account of their interrelation. He shows how the problems which arise in each of the first two Critiques, problems which are often seen as decisive objections to the Kantian philosophy, are recognized by Kant and dealt with in the third Critique. The *Critique of Judgement* is thus restored to the position in which Kant placed it, as the keystone of the critical arch.

But is is also remarkable, at first sight, that such a work should be written by, of all people, Gilles Deleuze. It is difficult to think of two philosophers more apparently opposite than old Immanuel Kant, 'the great Chinaman of Königsberg', and Gilles Deleuze, the Parisian artist of nomadic intensities. Yet, for Deleuze, it was precisely this opposition that was the fascination. Ten years ago Deleuze contrasted this book with his other work on the history of philosophy, as follows: 'My book on Kant is different, I like it very much, I wrote it as a book on an enemy, in it I was trying to show how he works, what his mechanisms are – the court of Reason, measured use of the faculties, a submissiveness which is all the more hypocritical as we are called legislators' (Lettre à Michel Cressole, p. 110). The fascination has continued over the years and has become more complex. In 1978 Deleuze gave a number of seminars on Kant, some of which are briefly summarized in the Preface written specially for this translation. In those seminars Deleuze still kept his distance from Kant, speaking of the 'fog of the north' and the 'suffocating atmosphere' of his work (Seminar of 14 March 1978), but something has also changed. Kant is now almost a Nietzschean, an 'inventor of concepts'. This resolutely anti-dialectical Kant, the 'fanatic of the formal concept', can already be discerned in the dry and sober pages of this 'introduction'.

In translating this work we have endeavoured to use, wherever possible, the familiar terminology of the English Kant translations. But the fact that we are dealing with a French text which is analysing a German original has caused occasional difficulties. Whenever German is translated into French or English it is always difficult to know when to retain capital letters for nouns. We have, in general, not attempted to impose any consistency on the use of capitals in the French. In one case we have felt it necessary to modify systematically the usual translations of Kant. The terms 'letzte Zweck' and 'Endzwecke' in the *Critique of Judgement* are rendered as 'ultimate end' and 'final end' by Meredith. We have preferred 'last end' and 'final end'. The French is 'fin dernière' and 'but final'. Modifications in the English translation used are indicated with an asterisk. We would like to thank Alan Montefiore (who has been pressing for a translation of this book for many years), Linda Zuck (whose idea it was, again, and who gave invaluable assistance) and Martin Joughin (an inspiration). The translation is dedicated to our parents.

H.R.E. Tomlinson
Barbara Habberjam

Abbreviations

CPR	*Critique of Pure Reason* (1781), trans. Norman Kemp Smith (Macmillan, 1964). References to the original first or second edition (A or B).
CPrR	*Critique of Practical Reason* (1788), trans. Lewis White Beck (Bobbs-Merrill, 1956). First reference: Prussian Academy edition of Kant's works (vol. V). Second reference: this translation.
CJ	*Critique of Judgement* (1790), trans. James Creed Meredith (Oxford University Press, 1973). First reference: Prussian Academy edition of Kant's works (vol. V). Second reference: this translation.
GMM	*Groundwork of the Metaphysics of Morals* (1785), trans. H. J. Paton (as *The Moral Law*; Hutchinson, 1972). First reference: original second edition. Second reference: this translation.
IUH	'Idea for a Universal History from a Cosmopolitan Point of View' (1784), trans. Lewis White Beck, in *Kant on History* (Bobbs-Merrill, 1963).

Introduction: The Transcendental Method

Reason according to Kant

Kant defines philosophy as 'the science of the relation of all knowledge to the essential ends of human reason', or as 'the love which the reasonable being has for the supreme ends of human reason' (CPR and Opus postumum, A839/B867). The supreme ends of Reason form the system of *Culture*. In these definitions we can already identify a struggle on two fronts: against empiricism and against dogmatic rationalism.

In the case of empiricism reason is not, strictly speaking, a faculty of ends. These are referred back to a basic affectivity, to a 'nature' capable of positing them. Reason's defining characteristic is rather a particular way of realizing the ends shared by man and animals. Reason is the faculty of organizing indirect, oblique means; culture is trick, calculation, detour. No doubt the original means react on the ends and transform them; but in the last analysis the ends are always those of nature.

Against empiricism, Kant affirms that there are ends proper to culture, ends proper to reason. Indeed, only the cultural ends of reason can be described as absolutely final. 'The final end is not an end which nature would be competent to realize or produce in terms of its idea, because it is one that is unconditioned' (CJ para. 84 435/98).

Kant puts forward three kinds of argument here:

Argument from value: if reason were of use only to achieve the ends of nature, it is difficult to see how its value would be superior to simple animality. (Given that it exists, there is no doubt that it must have a natural utility and use; but it exists only in relation to a higher utility from which it draws its value.)

Argument from the absurd: if Nature had wanted . . . (If nature had wanted to achieve its own ends in a being endowed with reason, it would have been mistaken to rely on the reasonable in him rather than on instinct, both for means and end.)

Argument from conflict: if reason were merely a faculty of means, it is difficult to see how two sorts of ends could be opposed in man, as both animal and moral species (for example: I stop being a child from Nature's point of view when I become able to have children, but from culture's perspective I am still a child, since I have no job and still have a lot to learn).

Rationalism, for its part, indeed recognizes that a rational being pursues strictly rational ends. But, here, what reason recognizes as an end is still something external and superior to it: a Being, a Good or a Value, taken as a rule of will. Consequently there is less difference than might be supposed between rationalism and empiricism. An end is a representation which determines the will. In so far as the representation is of something external to the will, it hardly matters whether it is sensible or purely rational; in any case it determines the act of willing only through the satisfaction linked to the 'object' which it represents. For either a sensible *or a rational* representation:

> the feeling of pleasure, by virtue of which they constitute the determining ground of the will . . . is always the same. This sameness lies not merely in the fact that all feelings of pleasure can be known only empirically, but even more in the fact that the feeling of pleasure always affects one and the same life-force. (CPrR Analytic, Theorem II Remark I 21/23)

Against rationalism, Kant asserts that supreme ends are not only ends of reason, but that in positing them reason posits nothing other than itself. In the ends of reason, it is reason which takes itself as its own end. Thus there are *interests* of reason, but reason turns out to be the only *judge* of its own interests. The ends or interests of reason cannot be justified in terms of experience, or of any other authority outside or above reason. Kant casts doubt on all such empirical decisions and theological tribunals:

> all the concepts, nay, all the questions which pure reason presents to us, have their source not in experience, but exclusively in reason itself . . . since reason is the sole begetter of these ideas, it is under obligation to give an account of their validity or of their illusory dialectical nature. (CPR A763/B791).

An immanent Critique – reason as the judge of reason – is the essential principle of the so-called transcendental method. This method sets out to determine:

1 the true nature of reason's interests or ends;
2 the means of realizing these interests.

First sense of the word 'Faculty'

Every representation is related to something other than itself; both to an object and to a subject. We can distinguish as many *faculties of mind* as there are types of relations. In the first place, a representation can be related to the object from the standpoint of its agreement to or conformity with it: this case, the simplest, defines the *faculty of knowledge*. Secondly, the representation may enter into a causal relationship with its object. This is the *faculty of desire*: 'the faculty which, by virtue of its representations, becomes the cause of the reality of the objects of these representations'. (We may object that there are impossible desires; but, in this example, a causal relationship is still implied in the representation as such, although it comes up against another causality which contradicts it. The example of superstition shows that even consciousness of our own impotence 'cannot put a brake on our efforts') (CJ Intro. para.3). Finally, the representation is related to the subject, in so far as it affects the subject by intensifying or weakening its vital force. This third relationship defines the faculty of the *feeling of pleasure and pain.*

There is perhaps no pleasure without desire, no desire without pleasure, no pleasure or desire without knowledge . . . etc. But this is beside the point. It is not a matter of knowing the actual combinations. It is a matter of knowing whether each of these faculties – on the basis of the principle in terms of which it is defined – is capable of a *higher form*. We may say that a faculty has a higher form when it finds *in itself* the law of its own exercise (even if this law gives rise to a necessary relationship with one of the other faculties). In its higher form, a faculty is thus autonomous. The *Critique of Pure Reason* begins by asking: 'Is there a higher faculty of knowledge?', the *Critique of Practical Reason*: 'Is there a higher faculty of desire?', and the *Critique of Judgement*: 'Is there a higher form of pleasure and pain?'. (For a long time Kant did not believe in this last possibility.)

Higher Faculty of Knowledge

A representation on its own is not enough to form knowledge. In order to know something, we need not only to have a representation, but to be able to go beyond it: 'in order to recognize another representation as being linked to it'. Knowledge is thus a synthesis of representations: 'we think we can find a predicate B outside the concept A, a predicate which is foreign to this concept, but which we think we ought to attach to it'. We affirm something of the object of a representation which is not contained within it. Now, this synthesis presents itself in two forms. When it depends on experience it is *a posteriori*. If I say: 'This straight line is white', this involves two different determinations: not every straight line is white, and that which is, is not necessarily so.

In contrast, when I say: 'A straight line is the shortest distance', or: 'Everything which changes has a cause', I am performing an *a priori* synthesis: I am affirming B as being necessarily and universally linked to A. (B is thus itself an *a priori* representation: as for A, it may not be.) The characteristics of the *a priori* are universality and necessity. But the definition of *a priori* is: independent of experience. It is possible that the *a priori* can be applied to experience and, in certain cases, can be applied only to experience, but it does not *derive* from it. By definition there is no experience which corresponds to the words 'all', 'always', 'necessarily' . . . The *shortest* is not a comparative, or the result of an induction, but an *a priori* rule from which I produce a line as a straight line. Similarly, *cause* is not the product of induction, but an *a priori* concept on the basis of which I recognize in experience something which happens.

As long as the synthesis is empirical, the faculty of knowledge appears in its lower form: it finds its law in experience and not in itself. But the *a priori* synthesis defines a higher faculty of knowledge. This is in fact no longer governed by objects which would give a law to it; on the contrary, it is the *a priori* synthesis which attributes a property to the object which was not contained in the representation. The object itself must therefore be subjected to the synthesis of representation: it must be governed by our faculty of knowledge, and not vice versa. When the faculty of knowledge finds its own law in itself, it legislates in this way over the objects of knowledge.

This is why the determination of a higher form of the faculty of knowledge is at the same time the determination of an interest of Reason. 'Rational knowledge and *a priori* knowledge are identical', or synthetic *a priori* judgements are themselves the principles of what should be called 'the theoretical sciences of reason' (CPR Preface, CPrR Introduction 5). An interest of reason is defined by what reason is interested in, in terms of the higher state of a faculty. *Reason has a natural speculative interest: and it has it for objects which are necessarily subject to the faculty of knowledge in its higher form.*

If we now ask 'What are these objects?', we can see immediately that to reply 'things in themselves' would be contradictory. How could a thing, *such as it is in itself*, be subject to our faculty of knowledge and be governed by it? In principle, this can only happen to objects *as they appear*, that is to say, to 'phenomena'. (So, in the *Critique of Pure Reason*, while *a priori* synthesis is independent of experience, it applies only to the objects of experience.) Thus we can see that the speculative interest of reason bears naturally on phenomena, and only on them. Kant did not need lengthy arguments to reach this result: it is a starting point for the Critique; the real problem of the *Critique of Pure Reason* begins here. If there were only the speculative interest, it would be very doubtful whether reason would ever consider things in themselves.

Higher Faculty of Desire

The faculty of desire presupposes a representation which determines the will. But, this time, can it be sufficient to invoke the existence of *a priori* representations for the synthesis of the will and of the representation to be itself *a priori*? The problem here is really quite different. Even when a representation is *a priori*, it determines the will through the medium of a pleasure linked to the object which it represents. The synthesis thus remains empirical or *a posteriori*; the will is determined 'pathologically', the faculty of desire remains in a lower state. In order for the latter to attain its higher form, the representation must cease to be a representation of an *object*, even an *a priori* one. It must be the representation of a pure form. 'If all material of a law, i.e. every object of the will considered as a ground of its determination, is abstracted from it, nothing remains except the mere form of giving universal law' (CPrR Analytic, Theorem III 26/27). The faculty of desire is thus a higher faculty, and the practical synthesis which corresponds to it is *a priori* when the will is no longer determined by pleasure, but by the simple form of law. Then the faculty of desire no longer finds its law outside itself, in content or in an object, but in itself: it is said to be autonomous.[1]

In the moral law, it is reason by itself (without the intermediary of a feeling of pleasure or pain) which determines the will. There is thus an interest of reason corresponding to the higher faculty of desire: a *practical interest.* which is distinct from both empirical interest and speculative interest. Kant constantly emphasizes the fact that practical Reason is profoundly 'interested'. We can thus sense that the *Critique of Practical Reason* will develop in parallel with the *Critique of Pure Reason*: it is concerned primarily with knowing what the nature of this interest is, and what it bears upon. That is to say, once the faculty of desire finds its own law in itself, what does this legislation bear on? Which objects find themselves subject to the practical synthesis? Despite the parallelism of the questions, however, the reply here will be far more complex. We will therefore consider this reply later. (Moreover, we will not undertake an examination of the question of a higher form of pleasure and pain, as the sense of this question itself presupposes the two other Critiques.)

We need only draw attention to an essential thesis of the Critical Philosophy in general: there are interests of reason which *differ in nature*. These interests form an organic and hierarchical system, which is that of the ends of a rational being. All that matters to the rationalists is the speculative interest: in their view practical interests are merely derived from this. But this inflation of the speculative interest has two unfortunate consequences: the real ends of speculation are misunderstood, but, more importantly, reason is *restricted* to only one of its interests. Under the pretext of developing the speculative interest, reason's deeper interests are mutilated. The idea of a systematic plurality (and a hierarchy) of interests – in accordance with the first sense of the word 'faculty' – dominates the Kantian method. This idea is a true principle, principle of a system of ends.

Second sense of the word 'Faculty'

In the first sense, 'faculty' refers to the different relationships of a representation in general. But, in a second sense, 'faculty' denotes a specific source of representations. Thus there are as many faculties as there are kinds of representations. The simplest list, from the point of view of knowledge, is the following:

1 Intuition (particular representation which relates immediately to an object of experience, and which has its source in *sensibility*);
2 Concept (a representation which relates mediately to an object of experience, through the intermediary of other representations, and which has its source in *understanding*).
3 Idea (a concept which itself goes beyond the possibility of experience and which has its source in *reason*). (CPR Transcendental Dialectic, Book I Section I: The Ideas in General)

However, the notion of representation as it has been used so far remains vague. To be more precise, we must distinguish between *the representation* and *what is presented*. That which is presented to us is initially the object as it appears. Yet even the word 'object' is too much. What presents itself to us, or what appears in intuition, is initially the phenomenon as sensible empirical diversity (*a posteriori*). We can see that, in Kant, phenomenon means not appearance, but appearing.[2] The phenomenon appears in space and time: space and time are for us the forms of all possible appearing, the pure forms of our intuition or our sensibility. As such, they are in turn presentations; this time, *a priori* presentations. What presents itself is thus not only empirical phenomenal diversity in space and time, but the pure *a priori* diversity of space and time themselves. Pure intuition (space and time) is the only thing which sensibility *presents a priori*.

Strictly speaking, intuition, even if it is *a priori*, is not a *representation*, nor is sensibility a source of representations. The important thing in representation is the prefix: *re* -presentation implies an active taking up of that which is presented; hence an activity and a unity distinct from the passivity and diversity which characterize sensibility as such. From this standpoint we no longer need to define knowledge as a synthesis of representations. It is the representation itself which is defined as knowledge, that is to say as *the synthesis of that which is presented*.

We must distinguish between, on one hand, intuitive sensibility as a faculty of reception, and, on the other, the active faculties as sources of real representations. Taken in its activity, synthesis refers back to *imagination*; in its unity, to *understanding*; and in its totality, to *reason*. There are thus three active faculties which participate in synthesis, but which are also sources of specific representations when any one of them is considered in relation to any other: imagination, understanding, reason. Our constitution is such that we have one receptive faculty and three active faculties. (We can imagine other beings, constituted in other ways: for example a divine being whose understanding would be intuitive and would produce the manifold. But then all his faculties would join together in a superior unity. The idea of such a Being as a limit can inspire our reason, but does not express our reason or its position in relation to our other faculties.)

Relation between the two senses of the word 'Faculty'

Let us consider a faculty in its first sense: in its higher form it is autonomous and legislative; it legislates over objects which are subject to it; an interest of reason corresponds to it. The first question of the Critique in general was therefore: 'What are these higher forms, what are these interests, and to what do they relate?' But a second question arises: 'How does an interest of reason realize itself?' That is to say, what assures the subjection of objects, *how* are they subjected? What is really legislating in a given faculty? Is it imagination, understanding, or reason? We can see that once a faculty in the first sense of the word has been defined so that an interest of reason corresponds to it, we still have to look for a faculty in the second sense, capable of realizing this interest, or of supporting the legislative task. In other words, there is no guarantee that reason itself undertakes to realize *its own* interest.

Take, for example, the *Critique of Pure Reason*. This begins by discovering the higher faculty of knowledge, and therefore the speculative interest of reason. This interest bears on phenomena; indeed, not being things in themselves, phenomena may be subject to the faculty of knowledge, and must be in order for knowledge to be possible. But, on the other hand, we may ask what faculty, as a source of representations, ensures this subjection and realizes this interest? What faculty (in the second sense) legislates *in* the faculty of knowledge itself? Kant's famous reply is that only understanding legislates in the faculty of knowledge or in the speculative interest of reason. Thus reason does not look after its own interest: 'Pure reason abandons everything to understanding'. (CPR Transcendental Dialectic, Book I Section I; Transcendental Ideas).

The reply will evidently not be identical for each Critique. So, in the higher faculty of desire, thus in the practical interest of reason – it is reason itself which legislates, and does not leave the business of realizing its own interest to another.

The second question of the Critique in general involves yet another aspect. A legislative faculty, as a source of representations, does not suppress all use of the other faculties. When understanding legislates in the interest of knowledge, imagination and reason still retain an entirely *original* role, but in conformity with tasks determined by the understanding. When reason itself legislates in the practical interest, it is understanding in its turn which has to play an original role, in a framework determined by reason . . . etc. In each Critique understanding, reason and imagination enter into various relationships under the chairmanship of one of these faculties. There are thus systematic variations in the relationship between the faculties, depending on which interest of reason we consider. In short: to each faculty in the first sense of the word (faculty of knowledge, faculty of desire, feeling of pleasure or pain) there must correspond a certain relationship between faculties in the second sense of the word (imagination, understanding, reason). In this way the doctrine of faculties forms the real network which constitutes the transcendental method.

1 The relationship of the faculties in the *Critique of Pure Reason*

A priori and Transcendental

Necessity and universality are the criteria of the *a priori*. The *a priori* is defined as being independent of experience, precisely because experience never 'gives' us anything which is universal and necessary. The words 'all', 'always', 'necessarily' or even 'tomorrow' do not refer to something in experience; they do not derive from experience even if they are applicable to it. Now, when we 'know', we employ these words; we say *more* than is given to us, we *go beyond* what is given in experience. The influence of Hume on Kant has often been discussed. Hume, indeed, was the first to define knowledge in terms of such a going beyond. I do not have knowledge when I remark: 'I have seen the sun rise a thousand times', but I do when I assert: 'The sun will rise *tomorrow*'; '*Every time* water is at 100°C, it *necessarily* begins to boil.'

Kant asks first of all: What is the fact of knowledge (*Quid facti*)? The fact of knowledge is that we have *a priori* representations (which allow us to judge). Sometimes they are simple 'presentations': space and time, *a priori* forms of intuition, intuitions which are themselves *a priori*, and are distinct from empirical presentations or from *a posteriori* contents (for example, the colour red). Sometimes they are, strictly speaking, 'representations': substance, cause, etc.; *a priori* concepts which are distinct from empirical concepts (for example, the concept of lion). The question *Quid facti*? is the object of *metaphysics*. The fact that space and time are presentations of *a priori* intuitions is the subject of what Kant calls the 'metaphysical exposition' of space and time. The fact that the understanding can make use of *a priori* concepts (categories), which are deduced from the forms of judgement, is the object of what Kant calls the 'metaphysical deduction' of concepts.

If we go beyond that which is given to us in experience, it is by virtue of principles which are our own, necessarily *subjective* principles. The given cannot be the basis of the operation by which we go beyond the given. It is not, however, sufficient that we have principles, we must have the opportunity to exercise them. I say: 'The sun will rise tomorrow', but tomorrow will not become present without the sun actually rising. We would quickly lose the opportunity to exercise our principles if experience did not itself come to confirm and, as it were, give substance to our going beyond. The given of experience must therefore itself be subject to principles of the same kind as the subjective principles which govern our own moves. If the sun sometimes rose and sometimes did not;

> if cinnabar were sometimes red, sometimes black, sometimes light, sometimes heavy; if a man changed sometimes into this and sometimes into that animal form, if the country on the longest day were sometimes covered with fruit, sometimes with ice and snow, my empirical imagination would never find opportunity when representing red colour to bring to mind heavy cinnabar. (CPR A100–101)

> otherwise our empirical imagination would never find opportunity for exercise appropriate to its powers, and so would remain concealed within the mind as a dead and to us unknown faculty. (CPR A100)

We can see the point where Kant breaks with Hume. Hume had clearly seen that knowledge implied subjective principles, by means of which we go beyond the given. But these principles seemed to him merely principles of *human nature*, psychological principles of association concerning our own representations. Kant transforms the problem: that which is presented to us in such a way as to form a Nature must necessarily obey principles of the same kind (or rather, the *same principles*) as those which govern the course of our representations. The same principles must account for our subjective moves, and for the fact that the given submits itself to our moves. That is to say, the subjectivity of principles is not an empirical or psychological subjectivity, but a 'transcendental' subjectivity.

This is why a higher question follows the question of fact: the question of right; *Quid juris*? It is not enough to note that, in fact, we have *a priori* representations. We must still explain why and how these representations are necessarily applicable to experience, although they are not derived from it. Why and how is the given which is presented in experience necessarily subject to the same principles as those which govern, *a priori*, our representations (and is therefore subject to our *a priori* representations themselves)? This is the question of right. Representations which do not derive from experience are called '*a priori* representations'. The principle by virtue of which experience is necessarily subject to our *a priori* representations is called a 'transcendental' principle. This is why the metaphysical exposition of space and time is followed by a transcendental exposition, and the metaphysical deduction of the categories by a transcendental deduction. 'Transcendental' qualifies the principle of necessary subjection of what is given in experience to our *a priori* representations, and correlatively the principle of a necessary application of *a priori* representations to experience.

The Copernican Revolution

In dogmatic rationalism the theory of knowledge was founded on the idea of a *correspondence* between subject and object, of an *accord* between the order of ideas and the order of things. This accord had two aspects: in itself it impled a finality; and it demanaded a theological principle as source and guarantee of this harmony, this finality. But it is curious that, from a completely different perspective, Hume's empiricism had a similar outcome: in order to explain how the principles of Nature were in accord with those of human nature Hume was forced to invoke explicitly a pre-established harmony.

The fundamental idea of what Kant calls his 'Copernican Revolution' is the following: substituting the principle of a *necessary* submission of object to subject for the idea of a harmony between subject and object (*final* accord). The essential discovery is that the faculty of knowledge is legislative, or more precisely, that there is something which legislates in the faculty of knowledge (in the same way there is something which legislates in the faculty of desire). The rational being thus discovers that he has new powers. The first thing that the Copernican Revolution teaches us is that it is we who are giving the orders. There is here an inversion of the ancient conception of Wisdom: the sage was defined partly by his own submission, partly by his 'final' accord with Nature. Kant sets up the critical image in opposition to wisdom: we are the legislators of Nature. When a philosopher, apparently very unKantian, announces the substitution of *Jubere* for *Parere*, he owes more to Kant than he himself might think.[1]

It would seem that the problem of a subjection of the object could be easily resolved by a subjective idealism. But no solution is further from Kantianism. *Empirical realism* is a constant feature of the critical philosophy. Phenomena are not appearances, but no more are they products of our activity. They affect us in so far as we are passive and receptive subjects. They can be subject to us, precisely because they are not things in themselves. But how can they be subject to us when they are not produced by us? How can a passive subject have, on the other hand, an active faculty, such that the affections which it experiences are necessarily subject to this faculty? In Kant, the problem of the relation of subject and object tends to be internalized; it becomes the problem of a relation between subjective faculties which differ in nature (receptive sensibility and active understanding).

Synthesis and the Legislative Understanding

Representation means the synthesis of that which is presented. Synthesis therefore consists in the following: a diversity is represented, that is to say posed as contained in a representation. Synthesis has two aspects: apprehension, by means of which we pose the manifold as occupying a certain space and *a certain* time, by means of which we 'produce' different parts in space and time; and reproduction, by means of which we reproduce the preceding parts as we arrive at the ones following. Synthesis defined in this way does not bear only on diversity as it appears in space and time, but on the diversity of space and time themselves. Indeed, without it, space and time would not be 'represented'.

This synthesis, as both apprehension *and* reproduction, is always defined by Kant as an act of the imagination.[2] But the question is: can we say with complete accuracy, as we did above, that synthesis is sufficient to constitute knowledge? In fact knowledge implies two things which go beyond synthesis itself: it implies consciousness, or more precisely the belonging of representations to a single consciousness within which they must be linked. Now, the synthesis of the imagination, taken in itself, is not at all self-conscious (CPR A78/B103). On the other hand, knowledge implies a necessary relation to an object. That which constitutes knowledge is not simply the act by which the manifold is synthesized, but the act by which the represented manifold is related to an object (recognition: this is a table, this is an apple, this is such and such an object).

These two determinations of knowledge are profoundly connected. My representations are mine in so far as they are linked in the unity of a consciousness, in such a way that the 'I think' accompanies them. Now, representations are not *united* in a consciousness in this way unless the manifold that they *synthesize* is thereby related to the object in general. Doubtless we know only qualified objects (qualified as this or that by a diversity). But the manifold would never be referred to an object if we did not have at our disposal objectivity as a form in general ('object in general', 'object = x'). Where does this form come from? The *object in general* is the correlate of the 'I think' or of the unity of consciousness; it is the expression of the *cogito*, its formal objectivation. Therefore the real (synthetic) formula of the *cogito* is: I think myself and in thinking myself, I think the object in general to which I relate a represented diversity.

The form of the object does not derive from the imagination but from the understanding: 'I conceive of the understanding as a *special* faculty and ascribe to it the concept of an object in general (a concept that even the clearest consciousness of our intutition would not at all disclose).'[3] Indeed, all use of the understanding is developed from the 'I think'; moreover, the unity of the 'I think' 'is the understanding itself' (CPR B134 fn.). The understanding makes use of *a priori* concepts which are called 'categories'; if we ask how the categories are defined we see that they are both *representations of the unity of consciousness* and, as such, *predicates of the object in general*. For example, not every object is red, and one which is red is not necessarily so; but there is no object which is not necessarily substance, cause and effect of something else, in a reciprocal relationship with something else. Thus the category provides unity for the synthesis of imagination without which it would not procure for us any knowledge in the strict sense. In short, we can say what depends on the understanding: it is not synthesis itself, it is the unity of synthesis and the expressions of that unity.

The Kantian thesis is: phenomena are necessarily subject to the categories; so much so that, through the categories, we are the true legislators of Nature. But the initial question is: Why does the understanding (and not the imagination) legislate? Why does it legislate *in* the faculty of knowledge? In order to answer this question it is perhaps sufficient to comment on the terms in which it is posed. Clearly we could not ask: Why are phenomena *subject* to space and time? Phenomena are what appear, and to appear is to be immediately in space and time.

> Since only be means of such pure forms of sensibility can an object appear to us and so be an object of empirical intuition, space and time are pure intuition which contain *a priori* the condition of the possibility of objects as appearances'. (CPR A89/B121)

This is why space and time are the object of an 'exposition' and not of a deduction; and their transcendental exposition, compared to the metaphysical exposition, does not raise any special difficulty. Thus it cannot be said that phenomena are 'subject' to space and time: not only because sensibility is passive, but above all because it is immediate and because the idea of subjection implies, on the contrary, the intervention of a *mediator*, that is, a synthesis which relates phenomena to an active faculty which is capable of legislating.

It follows that the imagination is not itself a legislative faculty. The imagination embodies the mediation, brings about the synthesis which relates phenomena to the understanding as the only faculty which legislates in the interest of knowledge. This is why Kant writes: 'Pure reason leaves everything to the understanding – the understanding alone applying immediately to the objects of intuition, or rather to their synthesis in the imagination' (CPR A326/B383–4). Phenomena are not subject to the synthesis of the imagination; they are subjected by this synthesis to the legislative understanding. Unlike space and time, the categories as concepts of the understanding are thus made the object of a *transcendental deduction*, which poses and resolves the special problems of a subjection of phenomena.

This problem is resolved, in outline, as follows: (1) all phenomena are in space and time; (2) the *a priori* synthesis of the imagination bears *a priori* on space and time themselves; (3) phenomena are therefore necessarily subject to the transcendental unity of this synthesis and to the categories which represent it *a priori*. It is exactly in this sense that the understanding is legislative: doubtless it does not tell us the laws which particular phenomena obey from the point of view of their content, but it constitutes the laws to which all phenomena are subject from the point of view of their form, in such a way that they 'form' a *sensible Nature* in general.

Role of the Imagination

We can now ask what the legislative understanding does with its concepts, or its unities of synthesis. It *judges*: 'The only use which the understanding can make of these is to judge by means of them'.[4] We can also ask: What does the imagination do with its synthesis? According to Kant's famous answer, the imagination *schematizes*. We should therefore not confuse synthesis and schema in the imagination. Schema presupposes synthesis. Synthesis is the determination of a certain space and a certain time by means of which diversity is related to the object in general, in conformity with the categories. But the schema is a spatio-temporal determination which itself corresponds to the category, everywhere and at all times: it does not consist in an image but *in spatio–temporal relations which embody or realize relations which are in fact conceptual*. The schema of the imagination is the condition under which the legislative understanding makes judgements with its concepts, judgements which will serve as principles for all knowledge of the manifold. It does not answer the question: 'How are phenomena subject to the understanding?' but rather the question: 'How is the understanding *applied* to the phenomena which are subject to it?'

The fact that spatio–temporal relations can be adequate to conceptual relations (in spite of their difference in nature) is, Kant says, a deep mystery and a hidden art. But we should not conclude from this text that the schematism is the deepest act of the imagination, or its most spontaneous art. The schematism is an original act of the imagination: only the imagination schematizes. But it schematizes only when the understanding presides, or has the legislative power. It schematizes only in the speculative interest. When the understanding takes up the speculative interest, that is, when it becomes *determining*, then and only then is the imagination *determined* to schematize. We will see the consequences of this situation below.

Role of Reason

Understanding judges, but reason *reasons*. Now, following Aristotle's doctrine, Kant conceives of reasoning in a syllogistic way: a concept of the understanding being given, reason looks for a middle term, that is to say another concept which, taken in its full extension, conditions the attribution of the first concept to an object (thus *man* conditions the attribution of 'mortal' to Caius). From this point of view it is therefore in relation to the concepts of the understanding that reason exercises its peculiar talents: 'reason arrives at knowledge by means of acts of the understanding which constitute a series of conditions' (CPR A330/B387). But it is precisely the existence of *a priori* concepts of the understanding (categories) which poses a special problem. The categories are applicable to all objects of possible experience; in order to find a middle term which makes possible the attribution of an *a priori* concept to *all* objects, reason can no longer look to another concept (even an *a priori* one) but must form *Ideas* which go beyond the possibility of experience. This is, in a sense, how reason is induced, in its own speculative interest, to form transcendental Ideas. These represent the *totality of conditions* under which a category of relation may be attributed to objects of possible experience; they therefore represent something *unconditioned* (CPR Dialectic, Book I, Section 2). Thus we have the absolute subject (Soul) in relation to the category of substance, the complete series (World) in relation to the category of causality and the whole of reality (God as *ens realissimum*) in relation to the category of community.

Here again we see that reason plays a role of which it alone is capable; but its playing of this role is determined. 'Reason has . . . as its sole object, the understanding and its effective application' (CPR A644/B672). *Subjectively*, the Ideas of reason refer to the concepts of the understanding in order to confer on them a maximum of both systematic unity and extension. Without reason the understanding would not reunite into a whole the set of its moves concerning an object. This is why reason, at the very moment it abandons legislative power in the interest of knowledge to the understanding, nevertheless retains a role, or rather *receives in return*, from the understanding itself, an original function: the constituting of ideal foci outside experience towards which the concepts of the understanding converge (maximum unity); the forming of the higher horizons which reflect and contain the concepts of the understanding (maximum extension) (CPR Dialectic, Appendix).

> Pure reason leaves everything to the understanding – the understanding alone applying immediately to the objects of intuition or rather to their synthesis in the imagination. Reason concerns itself exclusively with absolute totality in the employment of the concepts of the understanding and endeavours to carry the synthetic unity which is thought in the category, up to the completely unconditioned. (CPR A326/B383–4)

Objectively as well, reason has a role. For the understanding can legislate over phenomena only from the point of view of form. Now, let us suppose that phenomena were subject to the unity of synthesis from a formal point of view, but that in their content they showed radical diversity: once again the understanding would no longer have the opportunity to exercise its power (this time, the material opportunity). 'We should not even have the concept of a genus, or indeed any other universal concept, and the understanding itself which has to do solely with such concepts would be non-existent' (CPR A654/B682–3). It is therefore necessary not only that phenomena should be subject to the categories from the point of view of form, but also that their content correspond to, or symbolize, the Ideas of reason. At this level a harmony, a finality, is reintroduced. *But* here it is clear that the harmony between the content of phenomena and the Ideas of reason is simply postulated. It is not, indeed, a question of saying that reason legislates over the content of phenomena. It must presuppose a systematic unity of Nature; it must pose this unity as a problem or a limit, and base all its moves on the idea of this limit at infinity. Reason is therefore the faculty which says: 'Everything happens as if . . .' It does *not* say that the totality and the unity of conditions are given in the object, but only that objects allow us to tend towards this systematic unity as the highest degree of our knowledge. Thus the content of phenomena *does* correspond to the Ideas, and the Ideas to the content of phenomena; but, instead of necessary and determined subjection we have here only a correspondence, an indeterminate accord. The Idea is not a fiction, says Kant; it has an objective value, it possesses an object; but this object itself is 'indeterminate', 'problematic'. *Indeterminate* in its object, *determinable* by analogy with the objects of experience; bearing the ideal of an *infinite determination* in relation to the concepts of the understanding: these are the three aspects of the Idea. Thus reason is not content to reason in relation to the concepts of the understanding; it 'symbolizes' in relation to the content of phenomena.[5]

Problem of the Relationship between the Faculties: Common Sense.

The three active faculties (imagination, understanding, reason) thus enter into a certain relation, which is a function of the speculative interest. It is the understanding which legislates and which judges, but under the understanding the imagination synthesizes and schematizes, reason reasons and symbolizes, in such a way that knowledge has a maximum of systematic unity. Now, any accord of the faculties between themselves defines what can be called a *common sense*.

'Common sense' is a dangerous phrase, strongly tinged with empiricism. It must not therefore be defined as a special 'sense' (a particular empirical faculty). It designates, on the contrary, an *a priori* accord of faculties, or more precisely the 'result' of such an accord (CJ para. 40). From this point of view common sense appears not as a psychological given but as the subjective condition of all 'communicability'. Knowledge implies a common sense, without which it would not be communicable and could not claim universality. Kant will never give up the subjective principle of a common sense of this type, that is to say, the idea of a good nature of the faculties, of a healthy and upright nature which allows them to harmonize with one another and to form harmonious proportions. 'The highest philosophy in relation to the essential ends of human nature cannot lead further than does the direction granted to common sense.' *Even reason*, from the speculative point of view, possesses a good nature which allows it to be in agreement with the other faculties: the Ideas 'arise from the very nature of our reason; and it is impossible that this highest tribunal of all the rights and claims of speculation should itself be the source of deceptions and illusions' (CPR A669/B697).

Let us first of all consider the implications of this theory of common sense which must lead us to a complex problem. One of the most original points of Kantianism is the idea of a *difference in nature between our faculties*. This difference in nature appears not only between the faculty of knowledge, the faculty of desire and the feeling of pleasure and pain, but also between the faculties as sources of representations. Sensibility and understanding differ in nature, one as a faculty of intuition and the other as a faculty of concepts. Here again Kant opposes both dogmatism and empiricism which, in different ways, both affirmed a simple difference of degree (either a difference in clarity, based on the understanding; or a difference in liveliness, based on sensibility). But then, in order to explain how passive sensibility accords with active understanding, Kant invokes the synthesis and the schematism of the imagination which is applicable *a priori* to the forms of sensibility in conformity with concepts. But in this way the problem is merely shifted: for the imagination and the understanding themselves differ in nature, and the accord between these two active faculties is no less 'mysterious' (likewise the accord between understanding and reason).

It would seem that Kant runs up against a formidable difficulty. We have seen that he rejected the idea of a pre-established harmony between subject and object; substituting the principle of a necessary submission of the object to the subject itself. But does he not once again come up with the idea of harmony, simply transposed to the level of faculties of the subject which differ in nature? Doubtless this transposition is original. But it is not enough to invoke a harmonious accord of the faculties, nor a common sense as the result of this accord; the Critique in general demands a principle of the accord, as a genesis of common sense. (This problem of a harmony of faculties is so important that Kant tends to reinterpret the history of philosophy in the light of it:

> I am quite convinced that Leibniz, in his pre-established harmony (which he, . . . made very general) had in mind not the harmony of two different natures, namely sense and understanding, but that of two faculties belonging to the same nature, in which sensibility and understanding harmonize to form experiential knowledge.[6]

But this reinterpretation is itself ambiguous; it seems to indicate that Kant invokes a supreme finalist and theological principle *in the same way* as his predecessors: 'If we wanted to make judgements about their origin – an investigation that of course lies wholly beyond the limits of human reason – we could name nothing beyond our divine creator.'[7])

Let us nevertheless consider common sense in its speculative form (*sensus communis logicus*) more closely. It expresses the harmony of faculties in the speculative interest of reason, that is to say, under the chairmanship of the understanding. The accord of the faculties is here determined by the understanding, or – which amounts to the same thing – happens *under* the determined concepts of the understanding. We must anticipate that from the point of view of another interest of reason, the faculties enter into another relationship, under the determination of another faculty, in such a way as to form another common sense: for example a moral common sense under the chairmanship of reason itself. This is why Kant says that the accord of the faculties is capable of *several proportions* (depending on which faculty determines the relationship) (CJ para. 21). But each time we assume the perspective of a relationship or an accord which is already determined, it is inevitable that common sense should seem to us a kind of *a priori* fact beyond which we cannot go.

This is to say that the first two Critiques cannot resolve the original problem of the relation between the faculties, but can only indicate it and refer us to it as a final task. Every determinate accord indeed presupposes that the faculties are, at a deeper level, capable of a free and indeterminate accord (CJ para. 21). It is only at the level of this free and indeterminate accord (*sensus communis aestheticus*) the *we will be able to pose* the problem of a ground of the accord or a genesis of common sense. This is why we must not expect from the *Critique of Pure Reason* or from the *Critique of Practical Reason* the answer to a question which will take on its true sense only in the *Critique of Judgement*. As regards a ground for the harmony of the faculties, the first two Critiques are completed only in the last.

Legitimate Employment, Illegitimate Employment

1) Only phenomena can be subject to the faculty of knowledge (it would be contradictory for things in themselves to be subject to it). The speculative interest therefore naturally bears on phenomena; things in themselves are not the object of a natural speculative interest.
2) How precisely are phenomena subject to the faculty of knowledge and to what are they subject in this faculty? They are subject, through the synthesis of the imagination, to the understanding and to its concepts. It is therefore the understanding which legislates in the faculty of knowledge. If reason is, in this way, led to let understanding look after its own speculative interest, this is because it is not itself applicable to phenomena and forms Ideas which go beyond the possibility of experience.
3) The understanding legislates over phenomena from the point of view of their form. As such it is applicable, and must be exclusively applicable, to that which is subject to it: it gives us no knowledge whatsoever of things as they are in themselves.

This exposition does not take account of one of the fundamental themes of the *Critique of Pure Reason*. In many ways understanding and reason are deeply tormented by the ambition to make things in themselves known to us. Kant constantly returns to the theme that there are *internal illusions* and *illegitimate uses* of faculties. The imagination sometimes dreams rather than schematizes. Moreover, instead of applying itself exclusively to phenomena ('experimental employment') the understanding sometimes claims to apply its concepts to things as they are in themselves ('transcendental employment'). But this is still not the most serious problem. Instead of applying itself to the concepts of the understanding ('immanent or regulative employment'), reason may claim to be directly applicable to objects, and wish to legislate in the domain of knowledge ('transcendent or constitutive employment'). Why is this the most serious problem? The transcendental employment of the understanding presupposes only that it abstracts itself from its relation to the imagination. Now, this abstraction would have only negative effects were the understanding not pushed by reason, which gives it the illusion of a positive domain to conquer outside experience. As Kant says, the transcendental employment of the understanding derives simply from the fact that it *neglects* its own limits, whilst the transcendent employment of reason *enjoins* us to exceed the bounds of the understanding (CPR Dialectic, 'Transcendental Illusion').

It is in this sense that the *Critique of the Pure Reason* deserves its title: Kant exposes the speculative illusions of Reason, the false problems into which it leads us concerning the soul, the world and God. Kant substitutes, for the traditional concept of *error* (error as product in the mind of an external determinism), that of *false problems* and *internal illusions*. These illusions are said to be inevitable and even to result from the nature of reason (CPR Dialectic, 'The Dialectical Inferences of Pure Reason' and 'Appendix'). All Critique can do is to exorcise the effects of illusion on knowledge itself, but it cannot prevent its formation in the faculty of knowledge.

We are now touching on a problem which fully concerns the Critique of pure Reason. How can the idea of illusions internal to reason or of the illegitimate employment of the faculties be reconciled with another idea, no less essential to Kantianism: the idea that our faculties (*including reason*) are endowed with a good nature, and harmonize with one another in the speculative interest? On the one hand, we are told that the speculative interest of reason bears naturally and exclusively on phenomena and on the other that reason cannot help but dream of a knowledge of things in themselves and of 'interesting itself' in them from a speculative point of view.

Let us examine more carefully the two principal illegitimate uses. The transcendental use consists in the following: that the understanding *claims to know something in general* (therefore independently of the conditions of sensibility). Consequently, this something can be the thing as it is in itself; and it can only be thought of as suprasensible ('noumenon'). But, in fact, it is impossible for such a noumenon to be a positive object for our understanding. Our understanding does indeed have as a correlate the form of the object in general; but this is an object of knowledge only precisely in so far as it is qualified by a diversity with which it is endowed under the conditions of sensibility. Knowledge of the object in general which would not be restricted to the conditions of our sensibility is simply an 'objectless knowledge'. 'The merely transcendental employment of the categories is therefore really no employment at all, and has no determinate object, not even one that is determinable in its mere form' (CPR A247–8/B304).

The transcendent use consists in the following: that reason on its own claims to *know something determinate*. (It determines an object as corresponding to the Idea.) Despite having an apparently opposite formulation to the transcendental employment of the understanding, the transcendent employment of reason leads to the same result: we can determine the object of an Idea only by supposing that it exists *in itself* in conformity with the categories (CPR Dialectic, 'The Final Purpose of the Natural Dialectic of Human Reason'). Moreover, it is this supposition that draws the understanding itself into its illegitimate transcendental employment, inspiring in it the illusion of a knowledge of the object.

However good its nature, it is difficult for reason to have to pass on the responsibility for its own speculative interest and to deliver the legislative power to the understanding. But here we may note that the illusions of reason triumph above all, as long as reason remains in the *state of nature*. Now, we should not confuse reason's state of nature with its civil state, nor even with its natural law which is accomplished in the perfect civil state (CPR Doctrine of Method, 'Discipline of Pure Reason in Respect of its Polemical Employment'). The Critique is precisely the establishment of this civil state: like the jurist's contract, it implies a renunciation of reason from the speculative point of view. But when reason is renounced in this way the speculative interest does not stop being *its own* interest, and reason fully realizes the law of its own nature.

However, this answer is not sufficient. It is not sufficient to relate illusions or preversions to the state of nature, and good health to the civil state or even to natural law. For illusions subsist beneath natural law, in the civil and critical state of reason (even when they no longer have the power to deceive us). There is then only one way out: it is that reason, elsewhere, experiences an interest, itself legitimate and natural, for things in themselves, but an interest which is not speculative. Just as the interests of reason do not remain indifferent to one another but form a hierarchical system, it is inevitable that the shadow of the higher interest should be projected on to the lower. Then from the moment when it stops deceiving us, even illusion takes on a positive and well-established sense: it expresses in its own way the subordination of the speculative interest in a system of ends. Speculative reason would never have been interested in things in themselves if these were not, primarily and genuinely, the object of another interest of reason (CPR Doctrine of Method, 'The Ultimate End of the Pure Employment of our Reason'). We must therefore ask: What is this higher interest? (And it is precisely because the speculative interest is not the highest that reason can rely on the understanding in the legislation of the faculty of knowledge.)

2 The Relationship of the Faculties in the *Critique of Practical Reason*

Legislative Reason

We have seen that the faculty of desire is capable of a higher form: when it is determined not by representations of objects (of sense or intellect), nor by a feeling of pleasure or pain which would link this kind of representation to the will, but rather by the representation of a pure form. This pure form is that of a universal legislation. The moral law does not present itself as a comparative and psychological universal (for example: 'Do unto others! etc.). The moral law orders us to *think* the maxim of our will as 'the principle of a universal legislation'. An action which withstands this logical test, that is to say an action whose maxim can be thought without contradiction as universal law, is at least consistent with morality. The universal, in this sense, is a logical absolute.

The form of universal legislation is part of Reason. Indeed, understanding itself cannot think anything determinate if its representations are not those of objects restricted to the conditions of sensibility. A representation which is not only independent of all feeling, but of all content and of every sensible condition, is necessarily rational. But here reason does not reason: the consciousness of the moral law is a fact, 'not an empirical fact, but the sole fact of pure reason, which by it proclaims itself as originating law' (CPrR 31/31). Reason is thus that faculty which legislates immediately in the faculty of desire. In this form it is called 'pure practical reason'. And the faculty of desire, finding its determination *within* itself (not in a content or in an object), is strictly speaking called will, 'autonomous will'.

In what does the *a priori* practical synthesis consist? Kant's formulations of this vary. But to the question: 'What is the nature of a will sufficiently determined by the simple form of the law?' (thus independently of all conditions of sense or natural laws of phenomena), we must reply: It is a free will. And to the question: 'What law is capable of determining a free will as such?', we must reply: The moral law (as pure form of a universal legislation). The reciprocal implication is such that practical reason and freedom are, perhaps, one and the same. This, however, is not the real question. From the point of view of our representations, it is the concept of practical reason which leads us to the concept of freedom, as something which is necessarily linked to this first concept, which belongs to it and which nevertheless is not 'contained' in it. Indeed, the concept of freedom is not contained in the moral law, being itself an Idea of speculative reason. But this idea would remain purely problematic, limiting and indeterminate if the moral law had not taught us that we are free. It is only through the moral law that we know ourselves as free, or that our concept of freedom acquires an objective, positive and determinate reality. We thus find, in the autonomy of the will, an *a priori* synthesis which gives the concept of freedom an objective, determined reality by linking it necessarily to that of practical reason.

Problem of Freedom

The fundamental question is: Upon what does the legislation of practical reason bear? What are the beings or the objects which are subject to the practical synthesis? This question is no longer that of an 'exposition' of the principle of practical reason, but of a 'deduction'. Now we have a guiding thread: only free beings can be subject to practical reason. This legislates over free beings, or, more exactly, over the causality of these beings (the operation by which a free being is the cause of something). We will now turn our attention from the concept of freedom to *that which such a concept represents*.

In so far as we consider phenomena as they appear under the conditions of space and time, we find nothing which resembles freedom: phenomena are strictly subject to the law of a *natural causality* (as category of the understanding), according to which everything is the effect of something else on to infinity, and each cause is connected to a preceding cause. Freedom, on the contrary, is defined by its power to 'begin a state *spontaneously*. Such causality will not, therefore, itself stand under another cause determining it in time, as required by the law of nature' (CPR A533/B561). In this sense the concept of freedom cannot represent a phenomenon, but only a thing in itself, which is not given in intuition. Three elements lead us to this conclusion:

1 As it bears exclusively on phenomena, knowledge is forced in its own interest to posit the existence of things in themselves, as not being capable of being known, but having to be *thought* in order to serve as a foundation for sensible phenomena themselves. Things in themselves are thus thought as 'noumena', intelligible or suprasensible things which mark the limits of knowledge and return it to the conditions of sensibility. (CPR Analytic: 'The Ground of the Distinction of all Objects in general into Phenomena and Noumena').

2 In one case at least, freedom is attributed to the thing in itself and the noumenon must be thought as free: when the phenomenon to which it corresponds enjoys active and spontaneous faculties which are not reducible to simple sensibility. We have an understanding, and above all a reason; we are intelligences (CPR Dialectic, 'Explanation of the Cosmological Idea of Freedom'). As intelligences or rational beings, we must think of ourselves as members of an intelligible or suprasensible community, endowed with a free causality.

3 This concept of freedom, like that of noumenon, would still remain purely problematic and indeterminate (although necessary) if reason had no other interest apart from its speculative interest. We have seen that only practical reason determined the concept of freedom by giving it an objective reality. Indeed, when the moral law is the law of the will, the

> latter finds itself entirely independent of the natural conditions of sensibility which connect every cause to an *antecedent* cause: 'Nothing is antecedent to this determination of his will' (CPrR 97/101). This is why the concept of freedom, as Idea of reason, enjoys an eminent privilege over all the other Ideas: because it can be practically determined it is the only concept (the only Idea of reason) which gives to things in themselves the sense or the guarantee of a 'fact' and which enables us really to penetrate the intelligible world (CJ para. 91, CPrR Preface).

It seems, therefore, that practical reason, in giving the concept of freedom an objective reality, legislates in fact over the object of this concept. Practical reason legislates over the thing in itself, over the free being as thing in itself, over the noumenal and intelligible causality of such a being, over the suprasensible world formed by such beings. 'Suprasensible nature, so far as we can form a concept of it, is nothing else than nature under the autonomy of the pure practical reason. The law of this autonomy is the moral law, and it, therefore, is the fundamental law of suprasensible nature' (CPrR 43/44); 'The moral law is, in fact, a law of causality through freedom, and thus a law of the possibility of a suprasensible nature' (CPrR 47/49). The moral law is the law of our intelligible existence, that is to say, of the spontaneity and the causality of the subject as thing in itself. This is why Kant distinguishes *two kinds of legislation* and two corresponding *domains*: 'legislation by natural concepts' is that in which the understanding, determining these concepts, legislates in the faculty of knowledge or in the speculative interest of reason; its domain is that of phenomena as objects of all possible experience, in so far as they form a sensible nature. 'Legislation by the concept of freedom' is that in which reason, determining this concept, legislates in the faculty of desire, that is to say, in its own practical interest; its domain is that of things in themselves thought as noumena, in so far as they form a suprasensible nature. This is what Kant calls the 'great gulf' between the two domains (CJ Intro. para. 5. 2,99).

Beings in themselves, in their free causality, are thus *subject* to practical reason. But in what sense should 'subject' be understood? In so far as the understanding acts upon phenomena in the speculative interest, it legislates over something other than itself. But when reason legislates in the practical interest, it legislates over free and rational beings, over their intelligible existence, independent of every sensible condition. It is thus the rational being which gives itself a law by means of its reason. Contrary to what happens in the case of phenomena, the noumenon presents to thought the identity of legislator and subject. 'For it is not in so far as he is *subject* to the law that he has sublimity, but rather in so far as, in regard to this very same law, he is at the same time its *author* and is subordinated to it only on this ground' (GMM II, 86/101). This is what 'subject' means in the case of practical reason: the same beings are subjects and legislators, so that the legislator is here part of the nature over which he legislates. We belong to a suprasensible nature, but in the capacity of *legislative members*.

If the moral law is the law of our intelligible existence, it is in the sense that is is the form under which intelligible beings constitute a suprasensible nature. Indeed, it contains such a determining principle for all rational beings, which is the source of their systematic union (GMM II). On this basis we can understand the possibility of evil. Kant always maintains that evil has a certain relationship to sensibility. But it is no less based on our intelligible character. A lie or a crime are sensible effects, but they also have an intelligible cause outside time. It is for this reason that we ought not to identify practical reason and freedom: in freedom there is always a zone of *arbitrium liberum* (*libre-arbitre*) by means of which we can always choose against the moral law. When we choose against the law we do not cease to have an intelligible existence, we merely lose the condition under which this existence forms part of a nature and composes, with the others, a systematic whole. We cease to be subjects, but primarily because we cease to be legislators (indeed, we take the law which determines us from sensibility).

Role of the Understanding

It is thus in two very different senses that the sensible and the suprasensible each form a nature. Between the two Natures there is merely an 'analogy' (existence under laws). By virtue of its paradoxical character suprasensible nature is never completely realized, since nothing guarantees to a rational being that similar beings will bring their existence together with his, and will form this 'nature' which is possible only through the moral law. This is why it is not sufficient to say that the relation between the two Natures is one of analogy; one must add that the suprasensible can itself be thought of as a nature only *by analogy with* sensible nature (GMM II).

This can be clearly seen in the logical test of practical reason, the test to which we look to see if the maxim of a will can take on the practical form of a universal law. Firstly one considers whether the maxim can be set up as a universal *theoretical* law of a *sensible* nature. For example, if everyone told lies, promises would destroy themselves since it would be contradictory for anyone to believe them. The lie cannot therefore be a law of (sensible) nature. We can conclude from this that if the maxim of our will was a theoretical law of sensible nature, 'it would oblige everyone to truthfulness' (CPrR Analytic: 'Of the deduction of the principles of pure practical reason', 44/45). It can be deduced from this that the maxim of a mendacious will cannot without contradiction serve as a pure *practical* law for rational beings, resulting in their composition of a *suprasensible* nature. It is by analogy with the form of the theoretical laws of a sensible nature that we look to see if a maxim can be thought as the practical law of a suprasensible nature (that is to say, whether a suprasensible or intelligible nature is possible under such a law). In this sense, 'the nature of the sensible world' appears as 'the type of an intelligible nature' (CPrR Analytic: 'Of the Type of Pure Practical Judgement', 70/72).

It is clear that the understanding plays an essential role here. Indeed, we retain nothing of sensible nature which relates to intuition or to the imagination. We retain only 'the form of conformity to the law', as it is found in the legislative understanding. But we make use of this form, and of the understanding itself, following an interest and in a domain where the latter *is no longer* the legislator. For it is not the comparison of the maxim with the form of a theoretical law of sensible nature which constitutes the determining principle of our will (CPrR 70/72). Comparison is only a means by which we look to see whether a maxim 'adapts itself' to practical reason, whether an action is a case which fits the rule, that is to say, the principle of a reason which is now the only legislator.

This is how we encounter a new form of harmony, a new proportion in the harmony of the faculties. According to reason's speculative interest, the understanding legislates, reason reasons and symbolizes (it determines the object of its Idea 'by analogy' with the objects of experience). According to reason's practical interest, it is reason which legislates itself; the understanding judges or even reasons (although this reasoning is very simple and consists in a simple comparison), and it symoblizes (it extracts from natural sensible law a type for suprasensible nature), Now, in this new figure, we must continue to maintain the same principle: the faculty which is not legislative plays an irreplaceable role which it alone is capable of taking on, but to which it is determined by the legislative faculty.

How can the understanding by itself play a role in accord with a legislative practical reason? Let us consider the concept of causality: it is implied in the definition of the faculty of desire (relation of the representation to an object which it tends to produce).[1] It is thus implied in the practical employment of reason concerning this faculty. But when reason pursues its speculative interest, in relation to the faculty of knowledge, it 'abandons everything to the understanding': causality is assigned as category to the understanding, not in the form of a productive originating cause (since phenomena are not produced by us, but in the form of a natural causality or a connection which links sensible phenomena to infinity. On the contrary, when reason pursues its practical interest, it takes back from the understanding that which it had only lent to it in the perspective of another interest. Determining the faculty of desire in its higher form, it 'unites the concept of causality with that of freedom', that is to say, it gives the category of causality a suprasensible object (the free being as productive orginating cause) (CPrR, Preface). We may wonder how reason can take back that which it had abandoned to the understanding and, as it were, alienated into sensible nature. But, in fact, while the categories do not enable us to *know* objects other than those of possible experience, and while the categories do not form knowledge of the object independently of the conditions of possiblity, they nevertheless retain a purely logical sense in relation to non-sensible objects, and can be applied to them on condition that these objects are determined elsewhere and from a perspective other than that of knowledge.[2] Thus reason determines practically a suprasensible object of causality, and determines causality itself as a free causality, able to form a nature by analogy.

Moral Common Sense and Illegitimate Uses

Kant often reminds us that the moral law has no need at all for subtle arguments, but rests on the most ordinary or most common use of reason. Even the exercise of the understanding presupposes no previous instruction, 'neither science nor philosophy'. We must therefore speak of a moral common sense. Doubtless there is always a danger of understanding 'common sense' in an empiricist fashion, of making it a special sense, a feeling or an intuition: there can be no worse confusion about the moral law itself (CPrR Analytic: Scolie 2 of Theorem IV). But we define a common sense as an *a priori* accord of the faculties, an accord determined by one of them as the legislative faculty. Moral common sense is the accord of the understanding with reason, under the legislation of reason itself. We rediscover here the idea of a good nature of the faculties and of a harmony determined in conformity with a particular interest of reason.

But, no less than in the *Critique of Pure Reason*, Kant condemns illegitimate exercises or uses. If philosophical reflection is necessary it is because the faculties, in spite of their nature, generate illusions into which they cannot prevent themselves falling. Instead of 'symbolizing' (that is to say, making use of the form of natural law as a 'type' for moral law), the understanding comes to look for a 'schema' which relates the law to an intuition (CPrR Analytic: 'Of the type of pure practical judgement'. Moreover, instead of commanding without reconciling anything in the principle with sensible inclinations or empirical interests, reason comes to accomodate duty to our desires. 'From this there arises a *natural dialectic*' (GMM I, B23). We must therefore ask, once again, how we can reconcile the two Kantian themes: that of a natural harmony (common sense), and that of discordant exercises (non-sense).

Kant insists on a difference between the Critique of *pure* speculative Reason, and the Critique of practical reason: the latter is not a critique of 'pure' practical Reason. Indeed, in the speculative interest, reason cannot legislate itself (take care of its own interest): thus pure reason is the source of internal illusions as soon as it claims to assume a legislative role. In the practical interest, on the contrary, reason does not give anyone else the responsibility of legislating: 'where it is once demonstrated to exist, it is in no need of a critical examination' (CPrR Introduction, 16/16). It is not pure practical reason which needs a critique, or which is the source of illusions, but rather the impurity which is mixed up with it, in so far as empirical interests are reflected in it. Thus, to the critique of pure speculative reason there corresponds a critique of impure practical reason. Nevertheless, there remains something in common between the two: the so-called transcendental method is always the determination of an *immanent* employment of reason, conforming to one of its interests. The *Critique of Pure Reason* thus *condemns* the transcendent employment of a speculative reason which claims to legislate by itself; the *Critique of Practical Reason condemns* the transcendent employment of a practical reason which, instead of legislating by itself, lets itself be empirically conditioned (CPrR Introduction).

Nevertheless, the reader is entitled to wonder whether this famous parallel which Kant establishes between the two Critiques is an adequate reply to the question that was posed. Kant himself does not speak of a single 'dialectic' of practical reason, but uses the word in two quite different senses. He shows, in effect, that practical reason cannot prevent itself from setting up a link between *happiness* and *virtue*, but, in this way, falls into an antinomy. The antinomy consists in this: that happiness cannot be the cause of virtue (since the moral law is the sole determining principle of the good will), and that virtue seems no more able to be the cause of happiness (since the laws of the sensible world are in no way ordered in accordance with the intentions of a good will). Now, doubtless, the idea of happiness implies the complete satisfaction of our desires and inclinations. Nevertheless, one would hesitate to see in this antinomy (and above all in its second limb) the effect of a simple projection of empirical interests: *pure* practical reason itself demands a link between virtue and happiness. The antinomy of practical reason *does* express a more profound 'dialectic' than the previous one; it implies an internal illusion of pure reason.

The explanation of this internal illusion can be reconstituted as follows. (CPrR Dialectic: 'Critical solution of the antinomy'):

1 Pure practical reason excludes all pleasure or satisfaction as the determining principle of the faculty of desire. But when the law determines it, the faculty of desire experiences, for this very reason, a satisfaction, a kind of negative enjoyment expressing our independence from sensible inclinations, a purely intellectual contentment immediately expressing the formal accord of our understanding with our reason.
2 Now we confuse this negative enjoyment with a positive sensible feeling or even with a motive of the will. We confuse this active intellectual contentment with something felt, something experienced. (It is in this way that

the accord of the active faculties appears to the empiricist to be a special sense.) There is here an internal illusion that pure practical reason cannot itself avoid: 'there is always here an occasion for a subreption (*vitum subreptionis*) and, as it were, for an optical illusion in the self-consciousness of what one does in contradiction to what one feels, which even the most experienced person cannot entirely avoid' (CPrR Dialectic: (Critical solution of the antinomy', 116/121).

3 Thus, the antinomy rests on the immanent contentment of practical reason, on the inevitable confusion of this contentment with happiness. Then we sometimes think that happiness itself is the cause and motive of virtue, sometimes that virtue by itself is the cause of happiness.

If it is true, in accordance with the first sense of the word 'dialectic', that empirical interests or desires are projected into reason and render it impure, this projection has nevertheless a deeper internal principle in *pure* practical reason itself, in conformity with the second sense of the word 'dialectic'. The confusion of negative and intellectual contentment with happiness is an internal illusion which can never be entirely dissipated, but whose effect alone can be exorcised by philosophical reflection. It is also true that the illusion, in this sense, is only apparently contrary to the idea of a good nature of the faculties: the antinomy itself prepares a totalization which it is doubtless incapable of bringing about but which it forces us to seek, from the standpoint of reflection, as its own solution, or as the key to its labyrinth: 'the antinomy of pure reason, which becomes obvious in its dialectic, is in fact the most fortunate perplexity in which human reason could ever have become involved' (CPrR Dialectic: 'Of a dialectic of pure practical reason in general', 107/111).

Problem of Realization

Sensibility and imagination have, until now, had no role in moral common sense. This is not surprising as the moral law, in its principle as in its typical application, is independent of all schemas and conditions of sensiblity; since free beings and free causality are not the object of any intuition and since suprasensible Nature and sensible nature are separated by an abyss. There is indeed an action of the moral law on sensibility. But sensibility is considered here as feeling, not as intuition; and the effect of the law is itself a negative rather than a positive feeling, nearer to pain than pleasure. This is the feeling of respect for the law, determinable *a priori* as the only moral 'motive', but humbling sensibility rather than giving it a role in the relation of faculties. (It can be seen that the moral motive cannot be provided by the intellectual contentment of which we spoke earlier: this is not a feeling at all, but merely an 'analogue' of feeling. Only respect for the law provides such a motive; it presents morality itself as motive).[3]

But the problem of the relationship of practical reason and sensibility is neither resolved nor suppressed in this way. Respect serves rather as a rule preliminary to a task which remains to be positively fulfilled. *There is a single dangerous misunderstanding regarding the whole of practical Reason*: believing that Kantian morality remains indifferent to its own realization. In fact, the abyss between the sensible world and the suprasensible world exists only in order to be filled: if the suprasensible escapes knowledge, if there is no speculative use of reason which can carry us from the sensible to the suprasensible, on the other hand 'the latter is *meant* to influence the former – that is to say the concept of freedom is meant to actualize in the sensible world the end proposed by its laws' (CJ Introduction para. 2, 176/14). This is how the suprasensible world is the *archetypal world* (natura archetypa) and the sensible world the *ectypal world* (natura ectypa), because it contains the possible effect of the idea of the former' (CPrR Analytic: 'Of the deduction of the principles of pure practical reason,' A43/44). A free cause is purely intelligible; but we must realize that the *same being* is phenomenon and thing in itself, subject to natural necessity as phenomenon, source of free causality as thing in itself. Moreover, the *same action* the same sensible effect, relates on the one hand to a chain of sensible causes according to which it is necessary, but on the other itself relates, together with its causes, to a free Cause whose sign or expression it is. A free cause never has its effect in itself, since in it nothing happens or begins; *free causality only has sensible effects*. Thus practical reason, as law of free causality, must itself 'have causality in relation to phenomena' (CPR Dialectic). And the suprasensible nature that free beings form under the law of reason must be realized in the sensible world. It is in this sense that it is possible to speak of assistance, or opposition, between nature and freedom, depending on whether the sensible effects of freedom in nature do or do not conform to the moral law. 'Opposition or assistance is not between nature and freedom, but between the former as phenomenon and *the effects* of the latter as phenomena in the world of sense' (CJ Introduction para. 9, 195/37 fn.). We know that there are two types of legislation, thus two *domains* corresponding to nature and freedom, to sensible nature and to suprasensible nature. But there is only a single *terrain* (*terrain*), that of experience.

This is how Kant presents what he calls 'the paradox of method in a Critique of practical reason': a representation of an object can never determine the free will or precede the moral law; but by immediately determining the will, the moral law also determines objects as being in conformity with this free will. (CPrR Analytic, Chapter II: 'Of the concept of an object of pure practical reason'). More precisely, *when reason legislates in the faculty of desire, the faculty of desire itself legislates over objects*. These objects of practical reason form what is called the moral Good (it is in relation to the representation of the Good that we experience intellectual contentment). Now, 'the moral good is, in relation to the object, something suprasensible'. But it represents this object as something to be realized in the sensible world, that is to say 'as an effect possible through freedom'

(CPrR Analytic, Chapter II: 'Of the concept of an object of pure practical reason, A57/59). This is why, in its most general definition, the practical interest is presented as a relation of reason to objects, not in order to know them, but in order to *realize* them (CPrR 'Critical examination').

The moral law is entirely independent of intuition and of the conditions of sensibility; suprasensible Nature is independent of sensible Nature. Things which are good (*biens*) are themselves independent of our physical power to realize them, and are merely determined (in conformity with the logical test) by the moral possibility of willing the action which realizes them. Thus it is true that the moral law is nothing when separated from its sensible consequences; as is freedom when separated from its sensible effects. Is it sufficient therefore to present the law as legislating over the causality of beings in themselves, over a pure suprasensible nature? It would without doubt be absurd to say that phenomena are subject to the moral law as a principle of practical reason. Morality is not the law of sensible Nature; even the effects of freedom cannot contradict mechanism as the law of nature, since they are necessarily linked to each other in such a way as to form 'a single phenomenon' expressing the free cause. Freedom never produces a miracle in the sensible world. But if it is true that practical reason legislates only over the suprasensible world and over the free causality of the beings which compose it, it is no less true that all this legislation makes the suprasensible world something which must be 'realized' in the sensible world, and makes this free causality something which must have sensible effects expressing the moral law.

Conditions of Realization

It is still necessary that such a realization be possible. If it were not, the moral law would collapse of its own accord (CPrR Dialectic: 'The antinomy of practical reason'). Now, the realization of moral good presupposes an accord between sensible nature (*following its laws*) and suprasensible nature (following its law). This accord is presented in the idea of a proportion between happiness and morality, that is to say, in the idea of a Good Sovereign as the 'totality of the object of pure practical reason'. But if we ask how the Good Sovereign, in its turn, is possible and thus realizable, we come up against the antinomy: the desire for happiness cannot be the motive of virtue; but it also seems that the maxim of virtue cannot be the cause of happiness, since the moral law does not legislate over the sensible world and the latter is ruled by its own laws, which remain indifferent to the moral intentions of the will. However, this second direction leaves open a solution: that the connection of happiness with virtue is not immediate, but is made in the perspective of an infinite progress (the immortal soul) and through the intermediary of an intelligible author of sensible nature or of a 'moral cause of the world' (God). Thus the Ideas of the soul and of God are the necessary conditions under which the object of practical reason is itself posed as possible and realizable (CPrR Dialectic: 'On the postulates of pure practical reason').

We have already seen that freedom (as the cosmological Idea of a suprasensible world) received an objective reality from the moral law. Here we see that, in their turn, the psychological Idea of the soul and the theological Idea of the supreme being receive an objective reality under this same moral law. So the three great Ideas of speculative reason can be put on the same level, all being problematic and indeterminate from the point of view of speculation, but receiving a practical determination from the moral law. In this sense, and in so far as they are practically determined, they are called 'postulates of practical reason'; they form the object of a 'pure practical faith' (CPrR Dialectic: 'On assent arising from a Need of pure reason'). But, more precisely, it will be noted that practical determination does not bear on the three Ideas in the same way. Only the Idea of freedom is immediately determined by the moral law: freedom is therefore less a postulate than a 'matter of fact', or the object of a categorical proposition. The two other ideas as 'postulates' are merely conditions of the necessary object of a free will. 'That is to say that their possibility is proved by the fact that freedom is real' (CPrR Introduction; CJ para. 91).

But are the postulates the only conditions for a realization of the suprasensible in the sensible? There must still be conditions immanent to sensible Nature itself, which must establish in it the capacity to express or symbolize something suprasensible. They are presented under three aspects: natural finality in the content of phenomena; the form of the finality of nature in beautiful objects; the sublime in the formless in nature, by means of which sensible nature itself testifies to the existence of a higher finality. Now, in these last two cases, we see the *imagination* take on a fundamental role: whether it is freely exercised without depending on a determinate concept of the understanding; or whether it exceeds its own boundaries and feels itself to be unlimited, relating itself to the Ideas of reason. Thus the consciousness of morality, that is to say the moral common sense, not only includes beliefs (*croyances*), but the acts of an imagination through which sensible Nature appears as fit to receive the effect of the suprasensible. Imagination itself is thus really part of moral common sense.

Practical Interest and Speculative Interest

'To every faculty of the mind an interest can be ascribed, i.e. a principle which contains the condition under which alone its exercise is advanced' (CPrR Dialectic: 'Of the primacy of pure practical reason', 120/124). The interests of reason can be distinguished from empirical interests by what they bear upon in objects, but only in so far as these are subject to the higher form of a faculty. Thus the speculative interest bears upon phenomena in so far as they form a sensible nature. The practical interest bears upon rational beings as things in themselves, in so far as they form a suprasensible nature to be realized.

The two interests differ in nature, so that reason does not make speculative progess when it enters the domain which its practical interest opens up to it. *Freedom* as a speculative Idea is problematic, undetermined in itself; when it receives an immediate practical determination from the moral law, speculative reason gains no ground. It gains only 'in respect to the certitude of its problematic concept of freedom, to which objective, though only practical, reality is now indubitably given' (CPrR Analytic: 'Of the deduction of the principles of pure practical reason', 49/50). Indeed, we have no more knowledge of the nature of a free being than before; we have no intuition which can concern it. We merely know, through the moral law, that such a being exists and possessses a free causality. The practical interest is such that the relation of the representation to an object does not form a piece of knowledge, but designates something to be realized. Neither do *the soul and God*, as speculative Ideas, receive from their practical determination an extension from the standpoint of knowledge (CPrR Dialectic: 'On the postulates of pure practical reason in general').

But the two interests are not simply co-ordinated. It is clear that the speculative interest is subordinate to the practical interest. The sensible world would not be of speculative interest if, from the point of view of a higher interest, it did not testify to the possibility of realizing the suprasenible. This is why the Ideas of speculative reason itself have no other direct determination than the practical one. This can be clearly seen in what Kant calls 'faith'. Faith is a speculative proposition, but one which becomes assertoric only by the determination which it receives from the moral law. Thus faith is not related to a particular faculty, but expresses the synthesis of the speculative interest and the practical interest at the same time as the subordination of the former to the latter. This is the reason for the superiority of the moral proof of the existence of God to all the speculative proofs. For, as an object of knowledge, God is determinable only indirectly and analogically (as that from which phenomena draw a maximum of systematic unity); but, as object of belief, he acquires an exclusively practical determination and reality (moral author of the world) (CJ paras 87, 88).

An interest in general implies a concept of *end*. Now, if it is true that reason ends in the sensible nature that it observes, these material ends never represent a final end, any more than does this observation of nature: 'the existence of the world could not acquire a worth from the fact of its being known. A final end of the world must be presupposed as that in relation to which the contemplation of the world may itself possess a worth' (CJ para. 86, 492/108*). Final end, indeed, means two things: it is applied to beings which ought to be considered as *ends-in-themselves*, and which, on the other hand, should give sensible nature a *last end to realize*. The final end is thus necessarily the concept of practical reason, or of the faculty of desire in its higher form: only the moral law determines the rational being as end in itself, since it constitutes a final end in the employment of freedom, but at the same time determines it as the last end of sensible nature, since it commands us to realize the supra-sensible by uniting universal happiness with morality.

> For if creation has a last end at all we cannot conceive it other wise than as harmonizing necessarily with our moral faculty, which is what makes the concept of an end possible . . . the practical reason of these beings does not merely assign this final end, it also determines this concept in respect of the conditions under which a final end of creation can alone be thought by us. (CJ para. 88, 454/123).

The speculative interest finds ends only in sensible nature because, more profoundly, the practical interest implies the rational being as end in itself, and also as the last end of this sensible nature itself. In this sense it may be said that 'every interest is practical, and the very interest of speculative reason is only conditioned and is only complete in the practical usage'.[4]

3 The Relationship of the Faculties in the *Critique of Judgement*

Is there a Higher Form of Feeling?

This question means: are there representations which determine *a priori* a state of the subject like pleasure or pain? A sensation does not belong to this category; the pleasure or pain to which it gives rise (feeling) can be known only empirically. It does belong to this category, however, when the object's representation is *a priori*. Should we invoke the moral law as representation of a pure form? (Respect as the law's effect would be the higher state of pain; intellectual contentment the higher state of pleasure.) Kant's response is negative (CJ para. 12). For contentment is neither a sensible effect nor a special feeling, but an intellectual 'analogue' of feeling. And respect itself is an effect only in so far as it is a negative feeling; in its positivity it merges with, rather then derives from, the law as a motive. As a general rule, it is impossible for the faculty of feeling to attain its higher form when it finds its law itself in the lower or higher form of the faculty of desire.

What then would a higher pleasure be? It should not be linked to any sensible attraction (an empirical interest in the existence of the object of a sensation), nor to any intellectual inclination (a pure practical interest in the existence of an object of the will). It is only by being *disinterested* in its principle that the faculty of feeling can be higher. It is not the existence of the represented object which counts, but the simple effect of a representation on me. It could be said that a higher pleasure is the sensible expression of a pure *judgement*, of a pure operation of judging (CJ para. 9). The first aspect of this operation appears in aesthetic judgements of the type 'this is beautiful'.

But what representation can, in aesthetic judgement, have this higher pleasure as its effect? Since the material existence of the object remains indifferent, it is once again a case of the representation of a pure form. But this time it is a form of the object. And this form cannot simply be that of intuition, which relates us to materially existing external objects. In fact, 'form' now means this: the reflection of a singular object in the imagination. Form is the aspect of an object which the imagination reflects, as opposed to the material element of the sensations which this object provokes in so far as it exists and acts upon us. Kant then asks: Can a colour or a sound be called beautiful by themselves? Perhaps they would be if, instead of materially apprehending their qualitative effect on our senses, we were capable through our imagination of reflecting the vibrations of which they are composed. But colour and sound are too material, too entrenched in our senses to be reflected in our imagination in this way: they are the auxiliaries rather than the constituents of beauty. The essential thing is the design, the composition, which are precisely the manifestations of formal reflection (CJ para. 14).

In aesthetic judgement the reflected representation of the form causes the higher pleasure of the beautiful. We must then recognize that the higher state of the faculty of feeling has two paradoxical characteristics which are intimately linked. On the one hand, contrary to what happens in the case of the other faculties, the higher form here does not define any interest of reason: aesthetic pleasure is independent both of the speculative interest and of the practical interest and, indeed, is itself defined as completely disinterested. On the other hand, the faculty of feeling in its higher form is not legislative: all legislation implies objects on which it is exercised and which are subject to it. Now, aesthetic judgement is not only always particular, of the type 'this rose is beautiful' (the proposition 'roses in general are beautiful' implying a logical comparison and judgement) (CJ para. 8). More importantly, it does not even legislate over its singular object, since it remains completely indifferent to its existence. Kant therefore refuses to use the word 'autonomy' for the faculty of feeling in its higher form: powerless to legislate over objects, judgement can be only *heautonomous*, that is, it legislates over itself (CJ Intro. paras 4–5). The faculty of feeling has no *domain* (neither phenomena nor things in themselves); it does not express the conditions to which a kind of objects must be subject, but solely the subjective conditions for the exercise of the faculties.

Aesthetic Common Sense

When we say 'this is beautiful' we do not just mean 'this is pleasant': we claim a certain objectivity, a certain necessity, a certain universality. But the pure representation of the beautiful object is particular: the objectivity of the aesthetic judgement is therefore without concept or (which amounts to the same thing) its necessity and universality are subjective. Each time a determinate concept (geometric shapes, biological species, rational ideas) intervenes, aesthetic judgement ceases to be pure at the same time as the beauty ceases to be free (CJ para. 16; *pulchritudo vaga*). The faculty of feeling in its higher form can no more depend on the speculative interest than on the practical interest. That is why only pleasure is posited as universal and necessary in aesthetic judgement. We suppose that our pleasure is by rights communicable to or valid for everyone; we assume that everyone must experience this. This assumption, this supposition, is not even a 'postulate', since it excludes all determinate concepts (CJ para. 8).

However, this supposition would be impossible without some sort of intervention from the understanding. We have seen the role played by the imagination: it reflects a particular object from the point of view of form. In doing this it does not relate to a determinate concept of the understanding. But it relates to the understanding itself, as the faculty of concepts in general: it relates to an *indeterminate* concept of the understanding. In other words the imagination, in its pure freedom, is in agreement with the understanding in its non-specified legality.

One might say, as a last resort, that the imagination here 'schematizes without a concept' (CJ para. 35, 287/143). But schematism is always the act of an imagination which is no longer free, which finds its action determined in conformity with a concept of the understanding. In fact the imagination does something other than schematize: it displays its deepest freedom in reflecting the form of the object, it is 'as it were, at play in the contemplation of the figure' (CJ para. 16, 230/73*), it becomes productive and spontaneous imagination 'as originator of arbitrary forms of possible intuitions' (CJ General Remark on First Section of Analytic of the Beautiful, 240/86). Here, then, is an accord between the imagination as free and understanding as indeterminate. It is *a free and indeterminate accord* between faculties. This agreement defines a properly aesthetic common sense (taste). Indeed, the pleasure which we suppose to be communicable to, and valid for, everyone is nothing other than the result of this accord. Since it does not come into being under a determinate concept, the free play of imagination and understanding cannot be known intellectually, but only felt (CJ para. 9). Our supposition of a 'communicability of feeling' (without the intervention of a concept) is therefore based on the idea of a subjective accord of the faculties, in so far as this accord itself forms a common sense (CJ paras 39, 40).

It might be thought that aesthetic common sense *completes* the two earlier ones: in logical and in moral common sense understanding first, and then reason, legislate over and determine the function of the other faculties; now it would be the turn of the imagination. But this cannot be so. The faculty of feeling does not legislate over objects; it is therefore not *in itself* a faculty (in the second sense of the word) which is legislative. Aesthetic common sense does not represent an objective accord of the faculties (that is, a subjection of objects to a dominant faculty which would simultaneously determine the role of the other faculties in relation to these objects), but a pure subjective harmony where imagination and understanding are exercised spontaneously, each on its own account. Consequently aesthetic common sense does not complete the two others; *it provides them with a basis or makes them possible*. A faculty would never take on a legislative and determining role were not all the faculties together in the first place capable of this free subjective harmony.

But now we find ourselves faced with a particularly difficult problem. We explain the universality of aesthetic pleasure or the communicablity of higher feeling by the free accord of the faculties. But is it sufficient to assume this free accord, to suppose it *a priori*? Must it not be, on the contrary, *produced* in us? That is to say: should aesthetic common sense not be the object of a *genesis*, of a properly transcendental genesis? This problem dominates the first part of the *Critique of Judgement*; there are several complex points in its solution.

The Relationship between the Faculties in the Sublime

As long as we remain with aesthetic judgements of the type 'this is beautiful' reason seems to have no role: only understanding and imagination intervene. Moreover, it is a higher form of pleasure which is discovered, not a higher form of pain. But the judgement 'this is beautiful' is only one type of aesthetic judgement. We must examine the other type; 'this is sublime'. In the Sublime, imagination surrenders itself to an activity quite distinct from that of formal reflection. The feeling of the sublime is experienced when faced with the formless or the deformed (immensity or power). It is as if the imagination were confronted with its own limit, forced to strain to its utmost, experiencing a violence which stretches it to the extremity of its power. Imagination undoubtedly has no limit as long as it is a matter of *apprehending* (the successive apprehension of parts). But, in so far as it has to reproduce the previous parts as it arrives at the succeeding ones, it does have a limit to its simultaneous *comprehension*. Faced with immensity the imagination experiences the inadequacy of this maximum, and 'in its fruitless efforts to extend this limit, recoils upon itself' (CJ para. 26 252/100). At first sight we attribute this immensity, which reduces our imagination to impotence, to the natural object, that is to sensible Nature. But in reality it is *reason* which forces us to unite the immensity of the sensible world into a whole. This whole is the Idea of the sensible, in so far as this has as a substratum something intelligible or suprasensible. Imagination thus learns that it is reason which pushes it to the limit of its power, forcing it to admit that all its power is nothing in comparison to an Idea.

The Sublime thus confronts us with a direct subjective relationship between imagination and reason. But this relationship is primarily a *dissension* rather than an accord, a contradiction experienced between the demands of reason and the power of the imagination. This is why the imagination appears to lose its freedom and the feeling of the sublime seems to be pain rather than pleasure. But at the bottom of the dissension the accord emerges; the pain makes a pleasure possible. When imagination is confronted with its limit by something which goes beyond it in all respects it goes beyond its own limit itself, admittedly in a negative fashion, by representing to itself the inaccessibility of the rational Idea, and by making this very inaccessibilty something which is present in sensible nature.

> For though the imagination, no doubt, finds nothing beyond the sensible world to which it can lay hold, still this thrusting aside of the sensible barriers gives it a feeling of being unbounded; and that removal is thus a presentation of the infinite. As such it can never be anything more than a negative presentation – but still it *expands* the soul. (CJ para. 29, 'General Remark', 274/127)

Such is the – discordant – accord of imagination and reason: not only reason, *but also the imagination*, has a 'suprasensible destination'. In this accord the soul is felt as the indeterminate suprasensible unity of all the faculties; we are ourselves brought back to a focus, as a 'focal point' in the suprasensible.

It can then be seen that the imagination–reason accord is not simply assumed: it is genuinely *engendered*, engendered in the dissension. This is why the common sense which corresponds to the feeling of the sublime is inseparable from a 'culture', as the movement of its genesis (CJ para. 29). And it is within this genesis that we discover that which is fundamental to our destiny. In fact, the Ideas of reason are speculatively indeterminate, practically determined. This is the principle of the difference between the mathematical Sublime of the immense and the dynamic Sublime of power (the former brings reason into play from the standpoint of the faculty of knowledge, the latter from the standpoint of the faculty of desire) (CJ para. 24). So that, in the dynamic sublime, the suprasensible destination of our faculties appears as *that to which a moral being is predestined*. The sense of the sublime is engendered within us in such a way that it prepares a higher finality and prepares us ourselves for the advent of the moral law.

The Standpoint of Genesis

The difficulty is to find the principle of an analogous genesis for the sense of the beautiful. For in the sublime all is subjective, a subjective relationship between faculties; the sublime relates to nature only by projection, and this projection is carried out on what is formless or deformed in nature. In the beautiful too we are confronted by a subjective accord; but this develops from objective forms, so that a problem of deduction arises with regard to the beautiful which did not arise for the sublime (CJ para. 30). The analysis of the sublime has set us on the right track, since it showed us a common sense which was not merely assumed, but engendered. But a genesis of the sense of the beautiful poses a more difficult problem, since it requires a principle which would be objective in scope.[1]

We know that aesthetic pleasure is entirely disinterested, since it is not in any way concerned with the existence of an object. The beautiful is not the object of an interest of reason. *It may, however, be united synthetically with a rational interest.* Assuming this to be the case: the pleasure of the beautiful would not stop being disinterested, but the interest with which it were united might serve as a principle for a genesis of the 'communicability' or universailty of this pleasure; the beautiful would not stop being disinterested, but the interest with which it were united synthetically might serve as a rule for a genesis of the sense of the beautiful as common sense.

If this is indeed the Kantian thesis, we must find out which interest is united with the beautiful. The first suggestion to come to mind is an empirical social interest, which is so often linked to beautiful objects and which is capable of engendering a sort of taste or communicability of pleasure. But it is clear that the beautiful is linked to such an interest only *a posteriori* and not *a priori* (CJ para. 41). Only an interest of reason can fulfil the above requirements. But what can constitute a rational interest here? It cannot bear on the beautiful itself. It bears exclusively on the *aptitude which nature* possesses to produce beautiful forms, that is to say forms which are capable of being reflected in the imagination. (And nature presents this aptitude even where the human eye penetrates too seldom to reflect them properly; for example, in the depths of the ocean) (CJ para. 30.) The interest united with the beautiful does not therefore bear on the beautiful form as such, but on the *content* used by nature to produce objects capable of being reflected formally. It is not surprising that Kant, having initially said that colours and sounds were not in themselves beautiful, goes on to say that they are the object of an 'interest of the beautiful' (CJ para. 42). Moreover, if we look for the primary matter participating in the natural formation of the beautiful, we find it to be a fluid substance (the oldest state of matter), one part of which separates or evaporates while the rest rapidly solidifies (cf. the formation of crystals) (CJ para. 58). That is to say that the interest of the beautiful is neither an integral part of the beautiful, nor of the sense of the beautiful, but is concerned with the production of the beautiful in nature, and as such can serve as a principle in us for a genesis of the feeling of the beautiful itself.

The key question is as follows: What kind of interest is it? Until now we have defined the interests of reason by a type of objects which found themselves necessarily subject to a higher faculty. But there are no objects subject to the faculty of feeling.

The higher form of the faculty of feeling denotes only the subjective and spontaneous harmony of our active faculties, without any of these faculties legislating over objects. When we consider nature's material aptitude for producing beautiful forms we cannot deduce from this the necessary subjection of this nature to one of our faculties, but merely its *contingent accord* with all our faculties together (CJ Intro. 7). Moreover, it is fruitless to look for an end of Nature when it produces the beautiful; the precipitation of fluid matter is explicable in purely mechanical terms. Nature's aptitude thus appears as a power without aim, fortuitously adapted to the harmonious exercise of our faculties (CJ para. 58). The pleasure of this exercise is in itself disinterested; *however, we experience a rational interest in the contingent accord of nature's productions with our disinterested pleasure* (CJ para. 42). This is the third interest of reason: it is defined not by a necessary subjection but by a contingent accord of Nature with our faculties.

Symbolism in Nature

How is the genesis of the sense of the beautiful presented? It seems that the free materials of nature – colours, sounds – do not relate simply to the determinate concepts of the understanding. They overwhelm the understanding, they 'give food for thought' much more than that which is contained in the concept. For example, we do not merely relate colour to a concept of the understanding which would directly apply to it, we also relate it to a *quite different* concept which does not have an object of intuition on its own account, but which resembles the concept of the understanding because it posits its object by analogy with the object of the intuition. *This other* concept is an Idea of reason, which resembles the former only from the standpoint of reflection. Thus the white lily is not merely related to the concepts of colour and of flower, but also awakens the Idea of pure innocence, whose object is merely a (reflexive) analogue of the white in the lily flower (CJ paras 42,59). We can see here how the Ideas are the object of an indirect presentation in the free materials of nature. This indirect presentation is called *symbolism*, and has as its rule the interest of the beautiful.

Two consequences follow from this: the understanding itself sees its concepts enlarged in an unlimited way; the imagination is freed from the constraint of the understanding to which it remained subject in the schematism and becomes capable of reflecting form freely. The accord between imagination as free and understanding as indeterminate is therefore not merely assumed: it is in a sense animated, enlivened, engendered by the interest of the beautiful. The free materials of sensible nature symbolize the Ideas of reason; and in this way they allow the understanding to expand, the imagination to free itself. The interest of the beautiful bears witness to a *suprasensible unity* of all our faculties, to a 'focal point in the suprasensible', from which flows their free formal accord or their subjective harmony.

The indeterminate suprasensible unity of all the faculties, and the free accord which derives from it, are the deepest part of the soul. Indeed, when the accord of faculties finds itself determined by one of them (understanding in the speculative interest, reason in the practical interest) we assume that the faculties are *in the first place* capable of a free harmony (according to the interest of the beautiful) without which none of these determinations would be possible. But, on the other hand, the free accord of the faculties must *already* have involved reason, as that which is called upon to play the determining role in the practical interest or in the moral sphere. This is the sense in which the suprasensible destination of all our faculties is the pre-destination of a moral being; either the idea of the suprasensible as indeterminate unity of the faculties prepares the idea of the suprasensible as it is practically determined by reason (as principle of the ends of freedom); or the interest of the beautiful implies a disposition to be moral (CJ para. 42). As Kant says, *the beautiful itself is symbol of the good* (he means that the feeling of the beautiful is not a dim perception of the good, that there is no analytical relationship between the good and the beautiful, but that there is a synthetic relationship according to which the interest of the beautiful disposes us to be good, destines us for morality) (CJ para. 59). Thus the indeterminate unity and the free accord of the faculties do not merely constitute that which is *deepest* in the soul, but prepare the advent of that which is *most elevated*, that is to say the supremacy of the faculty of desire, and make possible the transition from the faculty of knowledge to this faculty of desire.

Symbolism in Art, or Genius

It is true that all the above (the interest of the beautiful, the genesis of the feeling of the beautiful, the relationship of the beautiful and the good) concerns only the beauty of nature. Everything rests, indeed, on the notion that nature has produced beauty (CJ para. 42). This is why the beautiful in art appears to have no relationship to the good, and why the sense of the beautiful in art seems to be incapable of having been engendered by a principle which destines us to morality. Whence the Kantian dictum: he who leaves a museum to turn towards the beauties of nature deserves respect.

Unless art too, in its own way, is amenable to a material and a rule provided by nature. But nature could proceed here only through an innate disposition of the subject. Genius is precisely this innate disposition by means of which nature gives art a synthetic rule and rich material. Kant defines genius as the faculty of *aesthetic Ideas* (CJ para. 57, 'Remark I'). At first sight an aesthetic Idea is the opposite of a rational Idea. The latter is a concept to which no intuition is adequate; the former an intuition to which no concept is adequate. But it is worth asking whether this inverse relationship is adequate to describe the aesthetic Idea. The Idea of reason goes beyond experience, either because there is no object which corresponds to it in nature (for example, invisible beings) or because it makes a simple phenomenon of nature into a spiritual event (death, love . . .). The Idea of reason thus contains something inexpressible. But the aesthetic Idea goes beyond all concepts because it creates the intuition of a nature other than that which is given to us: another nature whose phenomena would be true spiritual events, and whose events of the spirit, immediate natural determinations (CJ para. 49). It 'gives food for thought', it forces one to think. The aesthetic Idea is really the same thing as the rational Idea: it expresses what is inexpressible in the latter. This is why it appears as a 'secondary' representation, a second expression. In this respect it is very close to symoblism (the genius himself also proceeds by the extension of the understanding and the liberation of the imagination) (CJ para. 49). But instead of indirectly presenting the Idea in nature it expresses it secondarily, in the imaginative creation of another nature.

Genius is not taste, but it *animates* taste in art by giving it a soul or a content. There are works which are perfect as regards taste, but which lack soul, that is to say they lack genius (CJ para. 49). This is because taste itself is only the formal accord of a free imagination and an enlarged understanding. It remains dull and lifeless, and merely assumed, if it does not refer to a higher authority, as a content capable precisely of enlarging the understanding and freeing the imagination. In the arts, the accord of imagination and understanding is brought to life only by genius, and without it would remain incommunicable. Genius is a summons sent out to another genius; but taste becomes a sort of medium between the two, allowing a waiting period if the other genius is not yet born (CJ para. 49). Genius expresses the suprasensible unity of all the faculties, and expresses it as a living unity. It therefore provides the rule whereby the conclusions of the beautiful in nature may be extended to the beautiful in art. Therefore, the beautiful in nature is not the only symbol of the good; so is the beautiful in art by virtue of the synthetic and genetic rule of genius itself[2].

Kant thus adds to the *formal* aesthetic of taste a *material* meta-aesthetic, whose two main constituents are the interest of the beautiful and genius, and which bears witness to a Kantian romanticism. In particular, Kant adds to the aesthetic of line and composition – that is, of form – a meta-aesthetic of contents, colours and sounds. In the *Critique of Judgement* mature classicism and nascent romanticism are in a complex equilibrium.

We should not confuse the various ways in which, according

to Kant, the Ideas of reason can be presented in sensible nature. In the sublime the presentation is direct but negative, and done by projection; in natural sumbolism or in the interest of the beautiful the presentation is positive but indirect, and is achieved by reflection; in genius or in artistic symbolism the presentation is positive but secondary, and is achieved through the creation of another nature. We will see later that the Idea is capable of a fourth mode of presentation, the most perfect, in nature conceived as a system of ends.

Is Judgement a Faculty?

Judgement is always a complex operation which consists in subsuming the particular under the general. The man of judgement is always a man of skill: an expert, a doctor, a lawyer. Judgement implies a genuine gift, a flair (CPR Analytic: 'Transcendental Judgement in General'). Kant is the first to have thought of posing the problem of judgement at the level of its technicality, or of its own originality. In some well-known passages, Kant distinguishes two cases: either the general is already given, known, and all that is required is to apply it, that is to determine the individual thing to which it applies ('apodictical employment of reason', 'determining judgement'); or else the general poses a problem and must itself be found ('hypothetical employment of reason', 'reflective judgement') (CPR Dialectic, Appendix: 'The Regulative Employment of the Ideas of Pure Reason'). This distinction, however, is much more complicated than it seems: it should be interpreted as much from the point of view of examples as from that of signification.

A first mistake would be to believe that only reflective judgement involves inventiveness. Even when the general is given, 'judgement' is necessary to do the subsuming. Transcendental logic is undoubtedly distinct from formal logic in containing rules indicating the condition under which a given concept applies (CPR Analytic: 'Transcendental Judgement in General'). But these rules cannot be reduced to the concept itself: in order to apply a concept of the understanding we need the schema, which is an inventive act of the imagination, capable of indicating the condition under which individual cases are subsumed under the concept. The schematism itself is also an 'art', and the schema, one of 'cases which come under the law'. It would therefore be wrong to think that the understanding judges by itself: the understanding can only use its concepts for judging, but this use implies an original act of the imagination and also an original act of reason (this is why determining judgement appears, in the *Critique of Pure Reason*, as a particular exercise of reason). Every time Kant speaks of judgement as if it were a faculty it is to emphasize the originality of its act, the specificity of its product. But judgement always implies several faculties, and expresses the accord between them. Judgment is said to be determining when it expresses the accord of the faculties under a faculty which is itself determining: that is, when it determines an object in accordance with a faculty posited at the outset as legislative. Thus theoretical judgement expresses the accord of the faculties which determines an object in accordance with the legislative understanding. Similarly there is a practical judgement, which determines whether a possible action is a case subject to the moral law: it expresses the accord of understanding and reason under the chairmanship of reason. In theoretical judgement imagination provides a schema in accordance with the concept of the understanding; in practical judgement understanding provides a type in accordance with the law of reason. Saying that judgement determines an object is equivalent to saying that the accord of the faculties is determined, or that one of the faculties exercises a determining or legislative function.

It is therefore important to assess the examples which correspond to the two types of judgement, 'determining' and 'reflective'. Take a doctor who knows what typhoid (the concept) is, but does not recognize it in an individual case (judgement or diagnosis). We might be inclined to see in the diagnosis (which implies a gift and an art) an example of determing judgement, since the concept is supposed to be known. But in relation to a given individual case the concept itself is not given: it is problematic, or altogether indeterminate. In fact the diagnosis is an example of reflective judgement. If we look to medicine for an example of determining judgement, we must turn to a therapeutic decision: there the concept is effectively given in relation to an individual case, but what is difficult is its application (counter-indications in the patient, etc.).

In fact there is no less art or invention in reflective judgement. *But this art is distributed in a different way.* In determining judgement the art is as it were 'hidden'; the concept is given, whether it be concept of the understanding or law of reason; there is therefore a legislative faculty which directs or determines the original contribution of the other faculties, so that this contribution is difficult to evaluate. But in reflective judgement nothing is given from the standpoint of the active faculties; only a raw material presents itself, without really being 'represented'. All the active faculties are thus exercised freely in relation to it. Reflective judgement expresses *a free and indeterminate accord* between all the faculties. The art – which remained hidden, and as it were subordinate, in determining judgement – becomes manifest and exercises itself freely in reflective judgement. Through 'reflection' we may undoubtedly discover a concept which exists already; but reflective judgement will be all the purer for having no concept whatsoever for the thing which it freely reflects, or if the concept is (in a certain sense) enlarged, limitless, indeterminate.

In fact, determining judgement and reflective judgement are not like two species of the same genus. Reflective judgement manifests and liberates a depth which remained hidden in the other. But the other was also judgement only by virtue of this living depth. If this were not so it would be incomprehensible that the *Critique of Judgement* should have such a title, even though it deals only with reflective judgement. The point is that any determinate accord of the faculties under a determining and legislative faculty presupposes the existence and the possibility of a free indeterminate accord. It is in this free accord that judgement is not only original (this was already so in the case of determining judgement), but manifests the principle of its originality. According to this principle, despite the fact that our faculties differ in nature, they nevertheless have a free and spontaneous accord, which then makes possible their exercise under the chairmanship of one of them according to a law of the interests of reason. Judgement is always irreducible or original; this is why it can be called 'a' faculty (specific gift or art). It never consists in one faculty alone, but in their accord, whether an accord already determined by one of them playing a legislative role or, more profoundly, in a free indeterminate accord, which forms the final object of a 'critique of judgement' in general.

From Aesthetics to Teleology

When the faculty of knowledge is grasped in its higher form, the understanding legislates *in* that faculty; when the faculty of desire is grasped in its higher form, reason legislates in that faculty. *When the faculty of feeling is grasped in its higher form, it is judgement which legislates in that faculty.* (CJ Intro. 3, 9). This latter case is very different from the other two: aesthetic judgement is reflective; it does not legislate over objects, but only over itself; it does not express a determination of an object under a determining faculty, but a free accord of all the faculties with regard to a reflected object. We must ask whether there is another type of reflective judgement, or whether a free accord of the subjective faculties is manifested elsewhere than in aesthetic judgement.

We know that reason, *in its speculative interest*, forms Ideas whose sense is merely regulative. That is to say, they have no determinate object from the standpoint of knowledge, but endow the concepts of the understanding with a maximum of systematic unity. They nevertheless have a value which is objective, although 'indeterminate'; since they cannot endow concepts with a systematic unity without giving a similar unity to phenomena, considered in their content or their particularity. This unity, accepted as inherent in phenomena, is a *final unity* of things (a maximum of unity in the greatest possible variety, without the limit of this unity being clear). This final unity can be conceived of only by reference to a concept of *natural end*; in fact the unity of the manifold requires a relationship between this diversity and a determinate end, depending on which objects are related to this unity. In this concept of natural end, the unity is always merely assumed or presupposed, as reconcilable with the diversity of individual empirical laws (CJ Intro. 5; cf. CPR Dialectic: 'Appendix'). It does not therefore express an act by which reason would be legislative, and the understanding no longer legislates. The understanding legislates over phenomena, but only in so far as they are considered in the *form* of their intuition; its legislative acts (categories) therefore constitute *general* laws, and are exercised on nature as object of *possible* experience (every event has a cause . . . etc.). But understanding never determines *a priori* the *content* of phenomena, the detail of *real* experience or the *particular* laws of this or that object. These are known only empirically, and remain contingent in relation to our understanding.

Every law requires necessity. But the unity of empirical laws, from the standpoint of their particularity, should be conceived of as a unity which only an understanding *other than our own* could necessarily confer on phenomena. An 'end' is in fact defined by the representation of the effect as motive or foundation of the cause; the final unity of phenomena refers to an understanding which is capable of serving as its principle or substratum, in which the representation of the whole would be cause of the whole itself as effect (archetypal intuitive understanding defined as the supreme intelligent and intentional cause). But it would be an error to think that such an understanding exists in reality, or that phenomena are actually produced in this way: the archetypal understanding expresses a proper characteristic of our own understanding, namely our incapacity to determine the particular ourselves, our incapacity to conceive the final unity of phenomena according to any principle other than that of the intentional causality of a supreme cause (CJ para. 77). It is in this sense that Kant subjects the dogmatic notion of infinite understanding to a profound transformation: the archetypal understanding now only expresses to infinity the proper *limit* of our understanding, the point at which it ceases to be legislative in our speculative interest itself and relative to phenomena. 'By the peculiar constitution of my faculty of knowledge the only way I can judge of the possibility of those things and of their production is by conceiving for that purpose a cause working intentionally' (CJ para. 75 397–8/51*).

The finality of nature is thus linked to a twofold movement. On the one hand, *the concept of natural end derives from the Ideas of reason* (in so far as it expresses a final unity of phenomena): 'It subsumes nature under a causality that is only thinkable by the aid of reason' (CJ para. 74, 396/48). Nevertheless it is distinguishable from a rational Idea, since the effect which corresponds to this causality is effectively given in nature: 'Herein lies the point of difference between the concept of natural end and all other ideas' (CJ para. 77, 405/60*). As distinct from an Idea of reason, the concept of natural end has a given object; as distinct from the concept of the understanding, it does not determine its object. In fact, it intervenes to allow the *imagination* to 'reflect' on the object in an indeterminate way, so that the *understanding* 'acquires' concepts in accordance with the Ideas of *reason* itself. The concept of natural end is a concept of reflection which derives from the regulative Ideas: within it all our faculties are harmonized and enter a free accord which allows us to reflect on Nature from the standpoint of its empirical laws. Teleological judgement is thus a second type of reflective judgement.

Inversely, *on the basis of the concept of natural end we determine an object of the rational Idea*. The Idea doubtless does not have a determinate object in itself; but its object is determinable by analogy with the objects of experience. Now this indirect and analogical determination (which is perfectly reconcilable with the regulative function of the Idea) is possible only in so far as the objects of experience themselves display this final unity, in relation to which the object of the Idea must serve as principle, or substratum. Thus it is the concept of final unity or natural end which compels us to determine God as supreme intentional cause acting in the manner of an understanding. In this sense, Kant puts great emphasis on the need to move from a natural teleology to physical theology. The opposite move would be a false turning, 'turning Reason on its head' (the Idea would then have a constitutive rather than a regulative role; teleological judgement would be taken as determining). In nature we find no divine, intentional ends; on the contrary, we start from ends which are initially those of nature, and add to them the Idea of a divine intentional cause as condition of their comprehension. We do not impose ends on nature 'violently and dictatorily'; on the contrary, we reflect on the final natural unity, which is empirically known in diversity, in order to raise us to the Idea of a supreme cause determined by analogy (CPR Dialectic: Appendix, 'The Final Purpose of the Natural Dialectic of Human Reason', CJ paras 68, 75, 85). The combination of these two movements constitutes a new way of presenting the Idea; the final way which is distinct from those we have analysed above.

What is the difference between the two types of judgement, teleological and aesthetic? It must be borne in mind that aesthetic judgement already manifests a genuine finality. But it is a finality which is *subjective*, *formal*, *excluding any end* (whether objective or subjective). This aesthetic finality is subjective, since it consists in the free accord of the faculties among themselves.[3] It undoubtedly brings the form of the object into play, but the form is precisely that aspect of the object itself which the imagination reflects. Thus, objectively, it is a case of a pure subjective form of finality, ruling out any determinate material end (the beauty of an object may not be assessed in terms of its utility, nor of its internal perfection, nor of its relationship with any kind of practical interest) (CJ paras 11,15). It may be objected that Nature intervenes, as we have seen, by its material aptitude to produce beauty; in this sense we must indeed speak in respect of beauty, of a contingent accord of Nature with our faculties. This material aptitude is even an object of a particular 'interest' on our part. But this interest does not form part of the sense of the beautiful itself, although it gives us a principle according to which this sense may be engendered. Here the contingent accord of Nature and our faculties therefore remains in some sense external to the free accord of the faculties among themselves: nature only gives us the *external* opportunity 'for grasping the *internal* finality of the relation of our subjective faculties' (CJ para. 58, 350/220*). The material aptitude of nature does not constitute a natural end (which would contradict the idea of a finality without an end): 'it is we who receive nature with favour, and *not nature that does us a favour*' (CJ para. 58, 350/220).

Finality, in these different guises, is the object of an 'aesthetic representation'. Now it is clear that in this representation, reflective judgement appeals to particular principles in several ways: to the free accord of the faculties as foundation of this judgement (formal cause); to the faculty of feeling, as content or material cause, in relation to which judgement defines a particular pleasure as a higher state; to the form of finality without an end as final cause; and finally to the special interest for the beautiful as *causa fiendi* according to which the sense of the beautiful, which is rightfully expressed in aesthetic judgement, is engendered.

When we consider teleological judgement we are confronted with a completely different representation of finality. It is now a case of a finality which is *objective*, *material*, *implying ends*. That which dominates is the existence of a concept of natural end, expressing empirically the final unity of things in relation to their diversity. 'Reflection' therefore changes its meaning: it is no longer the formal reflection of the object without concept, but the concept of reflection through which the content of the object is reflected on. In this concept our faculties are freely and harmoniously exercised. But here the free accord of the faculties is still contained within the contingent accord of Nature and the faculties themselves. So, in teleological judgement, we must consider that Nature is genuinely doing us a favour (and when we return to aesthetics from teleology we consider that the natural production of beautiful things was *already* a favour of nature towards us) (CJ para. 67). The difference between the two judgements is the following: teleological judgement does not refer to particular principles (except in its use or application). It undoubtedly implies the accord of reason, imagination and understanding without the latter legislating; but this point at which understanding renounces its legislative claims is fully part of the *speculative interest* and remains within the sphere of the *faculty of knowledge*. This is why the natural end is the object of a 'logical representation'. There is undoubtedly a pleasure of reflection in teleological judgement itself; we do not experience pleasure in so far as Nature is necessarily subject to the faculty of knowledge, but we do experience it in so far as Nature agrees in a contingent way with our subjective faculties. But, even here, this teleological pleasure is mixed up with knowledge: it does not define a higher state of the faculty of feeling in itself, but rather an effect of the faculty of knowledge on the faculty of feeling (CJ Intro. 6).

It is easy to explain why teleological judgement does not refer to a particular *a priori* principle. It is because it is prepared by aesthetic judgement and would remain incomprehensible without this preparation (CJ Intro. 8). Formal aesthetic finality 'prepares' us to form a concept of end which is added to the principle of finality, completes it, and applies it to nature; it is reflection without concepts which itself prepares us to form a concept of reflection. Likewise there is no problem of genesis in relation to a teleological common sense; this is admitted or assumed in the speculative interest, and is a part of logical common sense, but in a way it is begun by aesthetic common sense.

If we consider the interests of reason which correspond to the two forms of reflective judgement, we rediscover the theme of a 'preparation', but in another sense. Aesthetics manifests a free accord of the faculties which is linked, in a certain way, to a special interest for the beautiful; now, this interest predestines us to be moral, thus preparing the advent of the moral law or the supremacy of the *pure practical interest*. Teleology, for its part, manifests a free accord of the faculties, this time in the *speculative interest* itself: 'under' the relationship of the faculties as it is determined by the legislative understanding, we discover a free mutual harmony of all the faculties, from whence knowledge draws a life of its own (we have seen that determining judgement, in knowledge itself, implied a living ground revealing itself only to 'reflection'). We must therefore consider that reflective judgement in general makes possible the transition from the faculty of knowledge to the faculty of desire, from the speculative interest to the practical interest, and prepares the subordination of the former to the latter, just as finality makes possible the transition from nature to freedom or prepares the realization of freedom in nature (CJ Intro. 3, 9).

Conclusion: The Ends of Reason

Doctrine of the Faculties

The three Critiques present a complete system of permutations. In the first place the faculties are defined according to the relationships of representation in general (knowing, desiring, feeling). In the second place they are defined as sources of representations (imagination, understanding, reason). When we consider any faculty in the first sense, a faculty in the second sense is called on to legislate over objects and to distribute their *specific* tasks to the other faculties: thus understanding legislates in the faculty of knowledge and reason legislates in the faculty of desire. It is true that in the *Critique of Judgement* the imagination does not take on a legislative function on its own account. But it frees itself, so that all the faculties together enter into a free accord. Thus the first two Critiques set out a relationship between the faculties which is determined by one of them; the last Critique uncovers a deeper free and indeterminate accord of the faculties as the condition of the possibility of every determinate relationship.

This free accord appears in two ways: *in* the faculty of knowledge, as a basis presupposed by the legislative understanding; and for itself, as a germ which destines us *to* legislative reason or to the faculty of desire. Therefore it is the deepest aspect of the soul, but not the highest. The *highest* aspect is the practical interest of reason, that which corresponds to the faculty of desire and which subordinates the faculty of knowledge or the speculative interest itself.

The originality of the doctrine of the faculties in Kant is as follows: their higher form never abstracts them from their human finitude any more than it suppresses their difference in kind. It is in so far as they are specific and finite that the faculties

– in the first sense of the word – take on a higher form and that the faculties – in the second sense – take on the legislative role.

Dogmatism affirms a harmony between subject and object and invokes God (possessing infinite faculties) in order to guarantee this harmony. The first two Critiques replace this with the idea of a necessary submission of the object to the 'finite' subject: to us, the legislators, in our very finitude (even the moral law is the fact of a finite reason). Such is the Copernican Revolution.[1] But, from this point of view, the *Critique of Judgement* seems to raise a special difficulty: when Kant uncovers a free accord beneath the determined relationship of the faculties, is he not simply reintroducing the idea of harmony and finality? And this in two ways: in the so-called 'final' accord between the faculties (subjective finality) and in the so-called 'contingent' accord of nature and the faculties themselves (objective finality).

Nevertheless, this is not the essential point. The essential point is that the *Critique of Judgement* gives us a new theory of finality, which corresponds to the transcendental point of view and fits perfectly with the idea of legislation. This task is fulfilled in so far as *finality no longer has a theological principle, but rather, theology has a 'final' human foundation*. From this derives the importance of the two theses of the *Critique of Judgement*: that the final accord of the faculties is the object of a special genesis; and that the final relationship between Nature and man is the result of a *human* practical activity.

Theory of Ends

Aesthetic judgement, unlike teleological judgement, does not refer to a principle which serves as an *a priori* foundation for its reflection. It must therefore be prepared by aesthetic judgement, and the concept of natural end presupposes primarily the pure form of finality without an end. But on the other hand, when we come to the concept of natural end, a problem is posed for teleological judgement which was not posed for aesthetic judgement; aesthetics left to taste the job of deciding which objects ought to be judged beautiful; teleology, on the contrary, requires rules to indicate the conditions under which a thing is judged according to the concept of natural end (CJ Intro. 8). The order of deduction is thus as follows: from the form of finality to the concept of natural end (expressing the final unity of objects from the standpoint of their content or of their particular laws); and from the concept of natural end to its application in nature (expressing, for reflection, the objects which should be judged according to this concept).

This application is a double one: we apply the concept of natural end to two objects, one of which is the cause and the other of which is the effect, in such a way that we introduce the idea of the effect into the causality of the cause (for example, sand as means in relation to pine forests). Or we apply it to a single thing as cause and effect of itself, that is to say, to a thing whose parts produce each other reciprocally in their form and their linkage (organized beings, organizing themselves). In this way we introduce the idea of a whole, not as cause of the existence of the thing ('for this would then be a product of art'), but as the foundation of its possibility as product of nature from the point of view of reflection. In the first case, the finality is external; in the second, internal (CJ paras 63–5). Now there are complex relationships between these two finalities.

On the one hand, external finality by itself is purely relative and hypothetical. In order for it not to be so, we would have to be capable of determining a *last end*; which is impossible through observation of nature. We observe only means which are already ends in relation to their cause, ends which are still means in relation to other things. We are thus forced to subordinate external finality to internal finality, that is to say, to consider that a thing is a means only in so far as the end which it serves is itself an organized being (CJ para. 82).

But on the other hand, it is doubtful whether internal finality does not, in turn, refer to a kind of external finality, raising the (apparently insoluble) question of a last end. Indeed, when we apply the concept of natural end to organized beings, we are led to the idea that the whole of nature is a system following the rule of ends.[2] From organized beings, we are sent back to external relations between these beings, relations which should cover the whole of the universe (CJ para. 82). But the point is that Nature could form such a system (instead of a simple aggregrate) only as a function of a last end. Now, it is clear that no organized being can constitute such an end: not even, above all, man as animal species. This is because a last end implies the *existence* of something as an end; but internal finality in organized beings concerns only their *possibility*, without considering whether their existence itself is an end. Internal finality only poses the question: Why do certain existing things have such or such a form? It does not even broach the other question: Why do things of this form exist? The only being which could be called a 'last end' is one which has the end of its existence *in itself*: the idea of a last end therefore implies that of the *final end*, which exceeds all our possibilities of observation in sensible nature and all the resources of our reflection (CJ paras 82,84).

A natural end is a foundation for possibility; a last end is a reason for existence; a final end is a being which possesses the reason for existence in itself. *But which one is the final end*? The only one who can be is the one who can develop a concept of ends; only man as rational being can find the end of his existence in himself. Does this mean man in so far as he looks for happiness? No, because happiness as an end leaves entirely untouched the question: Why does man exist (in a 'form' such that he strives to make his existence happy)? (CJ para. 86). Does it mean man as knower? The speculative interest, without doubt, constitutes knowledge as an end; but this end would be nothing if the existence of the one who knows were not a final end (CJ para. 86). In knowing we merely form a concept of natural end from the standpoint of reflection, not an idea of final end. Doubtless, with the help of this concept, we are capable of indirectly and analogically determining the object of the speculative Idea (God as the intelligent author of Nature). But 'why has God created Nature?' remains a question which is quite inaccessible to this determination. It is in this sense that Kant continually recalls the inadequacy of natural teleology as a foundation of theology: the determination of the Idea of God at which we arrive by this route merely gives us an opinion, not a belief (CJ paras 85,91 and 'General Remark on Teleology'). In short, natural teleology justifies the concept of a creative intelligent cause, but merely from the standpoint of the *possibility* of existing things. The question of a final end in the act of creating (What is the good of the *existence* of the world, and that of man himself?) exceeds all natural teleology, and cannot even be conceived of by it (CJ para. 85).

'A final end is simply a concept of our practical reason' (CJ para. 88, 454/124*). Indeed, the moral law prescribes an end without condition. In this end it is reason which takes itself as end, and freedom which necessarily gives itself a content as supreme and determined by the law. To the question 'Which one is the final end?', we must reply: man, but man as noumenon and suprasensible existence, man as moral being. '*With regard to man considered as moral being, one can no longer ask why he exists*; his existence contains in itself the supreme end . . .' (CJ para. 84*, 435/99). This supreme end is the organization of rational beings under the moral law, or freedom as reason for existence contained in itself in the rational being. What appears here is the absolute unity of a *practical finality* and an *unconditioned legislation*. This unity forms the 'moral teleology', in so far as practical finality is determined *a priori* in ourselves with its law (CJ para 87).

The final end is thus practically determinable and determined. Now we know how, according to the second Critique, this determination in turn entails a practical determination of the Idea of God (as *moral* author), without which the final end could not even be thought to be realizable. In any event, theology is always founded on a teleology (and not the other way round). But a moment ago we lifted ourselves from a natural teleology (a concept of reflection) to a physical theology (speculative determination of the regulative Idea, God as *intelligent* author). If this speculative determination is reconcilable with simple regulation, it is precisely in so far as it is entirely inadequate, remaining empirically conditioned and telling us nothing about the final end of divine creation (CJ para. 88). But now, on the contrary, we move *a priori* from a practical teleology (the practically determining concept of final end) to a moral theology (sufficient practical determination of the Idea of a *moral* God as the object of belief). It must not be thought that natural teleology is useless, for it impels us to look for a theology; but it is incapable of truly providing it. Neither must it be thought that moral theology 'completes' physical theology, nor that the practical determination of Ideas completes the analogical speculative determination. In fact, it supplements it, following *another interest of reason* (CJ: 'General Remark on Teleology'). It is from the standpoint of this other interest that we determine man as final end, and final end for the whole of divine creation.

History or Realization

The last question is: How is the final end also the last end of nature?' That is to say: How can man, who is only final end in his suprasensible existence and as noumenon, be the last end of *sensible nature*? We know that the suprasensible world must, in a certain way, be united with the sensible world: *the concept of freedom must realize the end imposed by its law in the sensible world.* This realization is possible under two kinds of conditions: divine conditions (the practical determination of the Ideas of reason which makes possible a good Sovereign as the accord of the sensible and the suprasensible worlds, of happiness and morality); and terrestrial conditions (finality in aesthetics and teleology, making possible a realization of the good Sovereign himself, that is to say a conformity of the sensible to a higher finality). The realization of freedom is thus also the accomplishment of the good sovereign: 'The union of the greatest well-being of rational creatures in the world with the highest condition of moral Good in it' (CJ para. 88). In this sense the final *unconditional* end is the last end of sensible nature, *under the conditions* which posit is as necessarily realizable and having to be realized in this nature.

In so far as the last end is nothing other than the final end, it is the object of a fundamental paradox: the last end of sensible nature is an end that this nature itself is not sufficient to realize (CJ para. 84). It is not nature which realizes freedom, but the concept of freedom which is realized or accomplished in nature. The accomplishment of freedom and of the good Sovereign in the sensible world thus implies an original synthetic activity of man: *History* is this accomplishment, and thus it must not be confused with a simple development of nature. The idea of last end implies a final relation of nature and man; but this relation is made possible only by natural finality. In itself and strictly, it is independent of this sensible nature and must be established, set up by man (CJ para. 83). The establishment of the final relation is the formation of a perfect civil constitution: this is the highest object of Culture, the end of history or the truly terrestrial good sovereign (CJ para. 83 and '*Idea for a Universal History*', Theses 5 – 8).

This paradox is easily explained. Sensible nature as phenomenon has the suprasensible as substratum. It is only in this substratum that the mechanism and finality of sensible nature are reconciled, the one concerning what is necessarily in it as object of sense, the other what is contingently in it as object of reason (CJ para. 77). It is therefore a *ruse* of suprasensible Nature, that sensible nature does not suffice to realize what is nevertheless 'its' last end; for this end is the suprasensible itself in so far as it must be accomplished (that is to say, have an effect in the sensible). 'Nature has willed that man should, by himself, produce everything that goes beyond the mechanical ordering of his animal existence, and that he should partake of no other happiness or perfection than that which he himself, independently of instinct, has created by his own reason' (IUH Thesis 3). Thus, whatever appears to be *contingent* in the accord of sensible nature with man's faculties is a supreme transcendental appearance, which hides a ruse of the suprasensible. But, when we speak of the effect of the suprasensible in the sensible, or of the realization of the concept of freedom, we must never think that sensible nature as phenomenon is *subject* to the law of freedom or of reason. Such a conception of history would imply that events are determined by reason, and by reason as it exists *individually* in man as noumenon; events would then manifest an 'individual rational purpose' of men themselves (IUH Introduction). But history, such as it appears in sensible nature, shows us the complete opposite: pure relations of forces, conflicts of tendencies, which weave a web of madness like childish vanity. Sensible nature always remains subject to laws which are its own. But if it is incapable of realizing its last end, it must none the less make possible the realization of this end, *in conformity with its own laws*. It is by the mechanism of forces and the conflict of tendencies (c.f. 'unsociable sociability') that sensible nature, in man himself, presides over the establishment of a Society, the only milieu in which the last end can be historically realized (IUH Thesis 4). Thus what appears to be a nonsense from the standpoint of the designs of an *a priori* individual reason can be a 'design of Nature' in order to ensure empirically the development of reason within the framework of the human *species*. History must be judged from the perspective of the species, and not of individual reason (IUH Thesis 2). There is thus a second ruse of Nature that we must not confuse with the first (both of them together constitute history). According to this second ruse, suprasensible Nature wanted the sensible to proceed according to its own laws, even in man, in order to be capable of receiving, finally, the effect of the suprasensible.

Notes

Introduction

1 For the *Critique of Practical Reason* we refer to the introduction by M. Alquié in the Presses Universitaires de France edition, and to the book by M. Vialatoux in the SUP 'Initiation Philosophique' series.
2 'I am not saying that bodies merely *seem* to be outside me . . . It would be my own fault, if out of that which I ought to reckon as appearance, I made mere illusion'. (CRP Aesthetic B69)

Chapter 1

1 *Translator's Note*: this is a reference to Chestov: see Gilles Deleuze, *Nietzche and Philosophy* (Athlone Press, 1983), p. 91.
2 CPR Analytic, *passim*; cf. 'There must therefore exist in us an active faculty for the synthesis of this manifold. To this faculty I give the title, imagination. Its action when immediately directed upon perceptions, I entitle apprehension'. (A120)
3 Letter to Herz, 26 May 1789 (*Kant's Philosophical Correspondence 1759–99*, ed. A Zweig, University of Chicago Press, 1967, p. 152).
4 CPR A68/B93. The question of whether *judgement* implies or forms a special faculty will be examined in Chapter 3.
5 The theory of symbolism appears only in the *Critique of Judgement*. But the 'analogy' which is described in the 'Appendix to the Dialectic' in the CPR is the first sketch of this theory.
6 Zweig, *op. cit.*, p. 154.
7 *Ibid.*

Chapter 2

1 CPrR Analytic: 'Of the right of pure reason to an extension in its practical use which is not possible to it in its speculative use'; 'In the concept of a will, however, the concept of causality is already contained'. (55/57)
2 CPrR Analytic: 'Of the right of pure reason to an extension . . .'
3 CPrR Analytic: 'The Incentives of Pure Practical Reason' (Respect is, without doubt, positive, but only 'by its intellectual cause').
4 CPrR Dialectic: 'On the Primacy of Pure Practical Reason' (cf. GMM III: 'An interest is that in virtue of which reason becomes practical . . . The logical interest of reason (interest in promoting its own insight) is never immediate, but presupposes ends for which reason can be employed'. (122/120)

Chapter 3

1 This accounts for the position of the analysis of the sublime in the *Critique of Judgement*.
2 Unlike para. 42, para. 59 ('Beauty as the symbol of morality') is as valid for art as it is for nature.
3 This is the origin, in para. 34 of CJ, of the expression 'mutual subjective finality' (286/141).

Conclusion

1 cf. the commentaries of M. Vuillemin on 'constituting finitude' in *L'Heritage Kantien et la Revolution Copernicienne*.
2 CJ para. 67. It is not strictly true that, according to Kant, finality is absolutely subordinated to internal finality. The opposite is true from another point of view.

Index

Index